Contents Table

Welcome & What You'll Learn

Welcome to the world of PowerShell! This book, "PowerShell Mastery: Command Your IT World," aims to be your indispensable guide to unlocking the full potential of Microsoft's powerful shell and scripting language. Whether you're an IT professional seeking streamlined automation, a power user desiring greater control over your system, or a curious learner ready to explore new technological frontiers, this book is designed to empower you.

Why PowerShell?

In our technology-driven landscape, the ability to automate repetitive tasks, manage systems efficiently, and interact with software at deeper levels is more valuable than ever. PowerShell stands out as an exceptional tool for achieving these goals. Here's why PowerShell deserves a place in your toolkit:

- **Object-Oriented Design:** Unlike traditional shells, PowerShell works natively with objects. This means you'll be manipulating structured data (like files, processes, or network connections) rather than just raw text, enabling more intuitive and flexible interactions.
- **Extensibility:** PowerShell is built on the .NET framework, giving you access to a vast ecosystem of libraries and modules. You can tap into the power of this framework to interact with virtually any software or system component.
- **Cross-Platform Compatibility:** PowerShell Core has brought PowerShell to Windows, macOS, and Linux, making it a truly versatile tool for managing systems across different environments.
- **Wide Application:** PowerShell's reach extends far beyond basic scripting. System administrators, network engineers, developers, and anyone who works closely with technology can leverage PowerShell to improve their workflow, saving time and effort.

What You'll Gain from This Book

This book adopts a structured and practical approach to PowerShell mastery. We'll progress from foundational concepts to advanced techniques, equipping you with the skills to:

- **Navigate the PowerShell Environment:** Become comfortable with the PowerShell console, integrated scripting environment (ISE), and discover valuable tools to enhance your experience.
- **Control the Flow of Data:** Master the art of working with objects, pipelines, sorting, filtering, and looping constructs to manipulate data according to your precise needs.

- **Handle and Transform Data:** Learn to format output, export data to various file formats (CSV, JSON, XML), and import external data sources to integrate PowerShell seamlessly into your workflow.
- **Create Reusable Functions and Scripts:** Break down complex tasks into modular functions and build robust PowerShell scripts, laying the foundation for efficient automation.
- **Automate System Administration:** Take charge of services, processes, scheduled tasks, event logs, and performance monitoring, turning PowerShell into your indispensable administrative assistant.
- **Harness Advanced PowerShell Techniques:** Power up your scripts by interacting with REST APIs, managing Azure services, integrating with other tools, building custom modules, and implementing robust error handling and debugging strategies for production-ready code.

How the Book is Structured

Our journey is divided into meticulously crafted sections:

- **Section 1: PowerShell Foundations** establishes a rock-solid foundation with a deep dive into PowerShell's syntax, data types, operators, cmdlets, aliases, and help systems.
- **Section 2: Object Manipulation in PowerShell** unlocks the superpower of object-oriented scripting, where you'll learn expert techniques to sort, filter, loop, and organize data.
- **Section 3: Handling, Storing, and Importing Data** focuses on input/output, file formats, and transforming data between PowerShell and external sources.
- **Section 4: Functions and Scripting** introduces the building blocks of modularity and automation, with detailed discussions on functions, parameters, and PowerShell scripting.
- **Section 5: Project - Automating File Organization with PowerShell** puts your newfound knowledge to the test! You'll design and execute a practical script to streamline file organization.
- **Section 6: PowerShell for System Administration** transforms you into a system administration pro as you learn to control services, processes, tasks, event logs, and more.
- **Section 7: PowerShell Automation and Advanced Techniques** ventures into the realm of REST APIs, Azure integrations, custom modules, error handling, and deployment techniques.

Let's Get Started!

Are you ready to embark on this exciting journey? Buckle up and let PowerShell transform the way you interact with your IT world!

Section 1:
PowerShell Foundations

Starting with PowerShell

Welcome to the first chapter of this journey into PowerShell mastery! Let's begin by laying the groundwork – understanding the different flavors of PowerShell, exploring its interfaces, and executing your first commands.

Flavors of PowerShell

Before we dive in, it's important to be aware that there are two main versions of PowerShell:

- **Windows PowerShell:** This is the classic version of PowerShell that ships with Windows operating systems. It's based on the older .NET Framework.
- **PowerShell Core:** This is a newer, cross-platform version of PowerShell built on .NET Core (now just .NET), compatible with Windows, macOS, and Linux.

While Windows PowerShell is still widely used, PowerShell Core is the future, offering better compatibility, improved performance, and a wider range of supported features. This book will focus primarily on PowerShell Core.

Introducing the PowerShell Interfaces

PowerShell offers several ways to interact with it. Let's introduce the most common ones:

1. **The PowerShell Console:** This is the classic command-line interface. It offers a quick and convenient way to execute PowerShell commands and try out simple scripts.
2. **PowerShell Integrated Scripting Environment (ISE):** The ISE offers a more comprehensive experience, providing a text editor, a

console pane for output, debugging capabilities, and enhanced syntax highlighting.

3. **Visual Studio Code with the PowerShell Extension:** VS Code, a popular code editor, provides a modern and versatile workspace when combined with the PowerShell extension. It offers intelligent code completion, an integrated terminal, and advanced debugging options.

Finding Your Way Around

Let's launch the PowerShell console to get familiar with its environment. Here's how to find it on a Windows system:

1. Press the Windows Key
2. Start typing "PowerShell"
3. You should see options for both "Windows PowerShell" and "PowerShell" (which is PowerShell Core).

Once you've opened the console, you'll be greeted with a command prompt, ready to accept input.

Your First Commands

PowerShell commands, known as cmdlets, follow a consistent `Verb-Noun` format. Let's start with some basics:

- **Get-Help:** The cornerstone of discovering new commands and understanding their usage. Try it out: `Get-Help Get-Process`
- **Get-Process:** Lists the currently running processes on your system.
- **Get-Service:** Displays the services installed on your machine.
- **Get-Command:** Lists available cmdlets. You can filter this list; for example, `Get-Command *process*` will show cmdlets related to processes.

A Word on Tab Completion: PowerShell features tab completion to save you time and reduce errors. If you start typing a cmdlet name or a file path and press the Tab key, PowerShell will cycle through possible matches.

PowerShell as a Calculator

You can use PowerShell for simple calculations! Try typing in these examples:

- `5 + 8`
- `12 * 7`
- `20 / 4`

Exiting PowerShell

To exit a PowerShell session, simply type `exit` and press Enter.

Additional Resources

- **Microsoft's PowerShell Documentation:**
  https://docs.microsoft.com/en-us/powershell/
- **The PowerShell Gallery:** A repository of community-created scripts and modules: https://www.powershellgallery.com/

Wrapping Up

In this chapter, you've become acquainted with the different versions of PowerShell, its interfaces, and essential cmdlets. You've even performed your first calculations! Get ready, because in the next chapter, we'll take a deeper look into navigating the PowerShell console effectively.

Navigating the PowerShell Console

In the last chapter, we dipped our toes into PowerShell by exploring its various flavors and trying out basic commands. Now, let's dive deeper and learn to navigate the PowerShell console with efficiency. Think of this as mastering the controls of the powerful machine you'll be commanding!

Understanding the Prompt

The PowerShell prompt is your gateway to interacting with the console. By default, it usually looks something like this:

PS C:\Users\YourUserName>

Let's break down what this tells us:

- **PS:** Indicates that you are in a PowerShell session.
- **C:\Users\YourUserName:** Represents your current working directory (or folder).
- **>:** The blinking cursor awaits your next command.

Changing Your Working Directory

You can use the cd cmdlet (short for "Change-Directory") to move between folders in PowerShell. Here's how:

- `cd <folderpath>`: Navigate to a specific folder. Example: cd C:\Windows\System32
- `cd ..`: Moves to the parent folder of the current location.
- `cd \`: Moves directly to the root of your current drive (usually C:).

Tip: Use tab completion! If you start typing a folder name and press Tab, PowerShell will try to autocomplete the path for you.

Directory Navigation Shortcuts

Here are some handy shortcuts to make navigating directories even faster:

- **cd ~:** Moves directly to your user's home directory.
- **cd -:** Takes you to the previous working directory.

Listing Files and Folders

The Get-ChildItem cmdlet, often aliased as ls or dir, is your essential tool for listing the contents of a directory.

- **Get-ChildItem:** Lists files and folders in the current directory.
- **Get-ChildItem <path>:** Lists contents of a specified directory. Example: Get-ChildItem C:\Windows

Clearing the Screen

Sometimes you might want to tidy up the console for better readability. The Clear-Host cmdlet (or its alias, cls) does the trick:

- **Clear-Host**

Customizing the Prompt

You can tailor the PowerShell prompt to display additional information. While advanced customization is possible, here's a simple yet useful trick:

1. Type $profile and press Enter. This shows the path to your PowerShell profile (a script that runs at startup).
2. If the file doesn't exist, use New-Item -Type File -Force $profile to create it.
3. Open the file in your preferred text editor (even Notepad will do).
4. Add a line like this to modify your prompt: function prompt { "CustomPS [$PWD]> " }
5. Save the file, restart PowerShell, and witness your new custom prompt!

Exploring Command History

PowerShell keeps a history of your previously entered commands. This is a fantastic time-saver! Here's how to utilize it:

- **Up/Down Arrow Keys:** Cycle through past commands.
- **F7:** Shows a popup window with your command history for easy searching.
- **Get-History:** Lists your command history
- **Invoke-History <id>** Reruns a command from your history by its ID (listed by Get-History)

Additional Resources

- **Microsoft Docs on Working with Files and Folders:** https://docs.microsoft.com/en-us/powershell/module/microsoft.powershell.management/
- **Exploring PowerShell's Profile:** https://docs.microsoft.com/en-us/powershell/module/microsoft.powershell.core/about/about_profiles

Let's Practice!

Open your PowerShell console and try:

1. Navigate to your user's "Documents" folder.
2. List the files inside this directory.
3. Create a new folder called "PowerShell_Scripts".
4. Clear the console.
5. Switch back to your previous working directory.

Next Up

Now that you're comfortable navigating the PowerShell console, we're ready to explore a fundamental concept: data types! Let's move on to Chapter 3.

Understanding Data Types: Part 1

In the world of programming, data comes in all shapes and sizes. Understanding data types is crucial because they determine how PowerShell stores, interprets, and allows you to interact with different kinds of information. Think of data types as the different containers you might use to organize your belongings; some are ideal for books, others for clothes, and others still for liquids.

What are Data Types?

A data type defines the following:

- **The kind of values a piece of data can hold:** Like numbers, text, dates, etc.
- **Available operations:** What you can do with that data (calculate, format, combine, etc.).
- **Memory allocation:** How much space PowerShell reserves to store the data.

Common Data Types in PowerShell

Let's explore some fundamental data types you'll encounter frequently:

1. **Strings:** These represent sequences of text characters. Enclosed in single or double-quotes.
   - Examples: `"Hello, World!"`, `'PowerShell'`
2. **Integers:** Whole numbers without decimal parts.
   - Examples: `10`, `-50`, `25000`
3. **Decimals (Floating-Point Numbers):** Numbers with decimal parts.
- Examples: `3.14159`, `-0.5`, `1234.567`
4. **Booleans:** Represent logical values of True or False.
   - Examples: `$true`, `$false`
5. **Arrays:** Ordered collections of elements. Can hold items of the same or different data types.
   - Example: `1, 2, 3, 4, 5` or `"one", "two", $true`
6. **Hashtables:** Unordered collections of key-value pairs

    ○ Example: `@{Name = "Alice"; Age = 30; City = "New York" }`

Discovering Data Types

Use the `GetType()` method to reveal the data type of any value or variable:

```
"Hello".GetType()    # This will output System.String
100.GetType()        # This will output System.Int32
$true.GetType()      # This will output
System.Boolean
```

Automatic Type Determination

PowerShell is quite forgiving! It usually figures out the data type automatically based on the information you provide. Here's an example:

```
$myNumber = 10      # PowerShell interprets this as
an integer
$myText = "Hello"   # PowerShell interprets this as
a string
```

Changing Data Types (Type Casting)

Sometimes, you'll need to convert data from one type to another. This is called type casting. Here's how it works:

```
[int]"123"        # Converts the string "123" to an
integer
[string]100       # Converts the integer 100 to a
string
[bool]"True"      # Converts the string "True" to a
boolean (True)
```

Important Considerations

- **Valid Conversions:** Be mindful that not all conversions make sense. Trying to convert "Hello" into an integer will result in an error.

- **Potential Data Loss:** When converting from a wider data type to a narrower type (e.g., decimal to integer), you might lose precision.

Practice Time!

1. **Experiment:** Use `GetType()` to discover the data types of different values like `3.14`, `"PowerShell is awesome!"`, `$false`.
2. **Casting:** Try converting the following:
   - The string "500" to an integer.
   - The number 15.75 to a string.

Coming Up…

In Part 2 of "Understanding Data Types," we'll delve into more complex data structures, dates and times, and how PowerShell's dynamic typing works behind the scenes.

Understanding Data Types: Part 2

In the previous chapter, we laid the groundwork for understanding basic data types in PowerShell. Now, let's go deeper by introducing some more complex data structures and exploring concepts like dates, times, and PowerShell's flexibility with data types.

More Complex Data Structures

1. **Dates and Times:** PowerShell has special ways to represent points in time:
   - **[DateTime] Objects:** These hold information about both date and time.
     - Example: Get-Date (Gets the current date and time)
     - You can format DateTimes, extract specific components (year, month, hour, etc.), and even perform calculations between dates.
2. **[PSCustomObject] Type:** Lets you create your own custom objects with properties. Here's a simple example:

```
$myObject = [PSCustomObject]@{
    Name = "John Doe"
    Email = "john.doe@example.com"
    Role = "IT Admin"
}
```

Dynamic Typing: Flexibility with a Catch

PowerShell often figures out data types for you, but this flexibility can sometimes lead to unexpected behavior if you're not careful. Let's see an example:

```
$result = "5" + 10
$result.GetType()    # Output: System.String
```

In the code above, you might expect $result to be 15. However, since "5" is a string, PowerShell treats the + operator as string concatenation, giving you the result "510".

Enforcing Data Types

To avoid surprises, you can be explicit about data types:

```
$result = [int]"5" + 10
$result.GetType()   # Output: System.Int32
```

Special Data Types

- **[Null]:** Represents the absence of a value. Used for unassigned variables or empty results. Example: $null
- **Enumerated Types (Enums):** Create custom data types with a defined set of named values. They make your code more readable! (We'll explore these in later chapters)

Practical Example: Parsing a CSV File

Let's see data types in action. Suppose you have a CSV (Comma-Separated Values) file named 'users.csv':

```
Name, Age, City
Alice, 30, New York
Bob, 25, London
Charlie, 40, Paris
```

Here's some PowerShell code to read this data:

```
$users = Import-Csv .\users.csv

# Each row becomes an object
$users[0].Name   #  Outputs: Alice
$users[1].Age    #  Outputs: 25 (Treated as a string
by default)

# Type Casting
[int]$users[1].Age + 5   # Now we can do math with
it!
```

Keep Experimenting

The best way to get comfortable with data types is to try the following:

1. **Type Exploration:** Use `GetType()` on various values and variables to uncover their underlying data types.
2. **CSV Fun:** Find a sample CSV file online and use `Import-Csv` to load it into PowerShell. Explore the objects it creates.

In the Next Chapter…

We'll switch gears and dive into the world of comparison operators, which allow you to compare values and make decisions in your PowerShell scripts. Let's get ready to control the flow!

Comparison Operators, Part 1

In programming, it's not just about manipulating data; you often need to make comparisons to guide the flow of your scripts. Comparison operators are the key to asking questions like "Is this value greater than that one?" or "Are these two items the same?"

Types of Comparison Operators

PowerShell offers a rich set of comparison operators:

- **Equality Operators**
  - **-eq** (Equal): Example: 5 -eq 5 (True)
  - **-ne** (Not Equal): Example: 5 -ne 10 (True)
  - **-gt** (Greater Than): Example: 10 -gt 7 (True)
  - **-ge** (Greater Than or Equal): Example: 5 -ge 5 (True)
  - **-lt** (Less Than): Example: 3 -lt 8 (True)
  - **-le** (Less Than or Equal): Example: 8 -le 10 (True)
- **Case-Sensitivity**

By default, string comparisons in PowerShell are *case-insensitive*. Use case-sensitive versions of the operators if needed (e.g., -ceq, -cne instead of -eq, -ne).

- **Match Operators**
  - **-like** (Wildcard matching): Example: "PowerShell" -like "*Shell" (True)
  - **-notlike** (Negated wildcard matching): Example: "PowerShell" -notlike "Linux" (True)
  - **-match** (Regular expression matching): For complex pattern matching (More advanced topic, we'll cover later)
  - **-notmatch** (Negated regular expression matching)

Working with Different Data Types

When comparing different data types, PowerShell implicitly tries to convert one of them to make the comparison possible. Here are some key points:

- **Numbers vs. Strings:** Numbers in quotes are treated as strings. 5 -eq "5" would be False.
- **Arrays and Scalars:** Comparing an array to a single value checks if that value exists within the array.

Examples

```
$age = 30
$name = "John Doe"

# Equality & Inequality
$age -eq 30  # True
$name -ne "Sarah"  # True

# Greater than / Less than
$age -gt 25  # True

# String Comparisons
"PowerShell" -like "*Shell"  # True
"Windows" -notlike "macOS"  # True
```

Applications: Conditional Logic

Comparison operators shine when combined with PowerShell's conditional statements, like if, else if, and else. Simple Example:

```
$diskFreeSpace = 20 # In Gigabytes

if ($diskFreeSpace -lt 10) {
    Write-Warning "Low disk space!"
} else {
    Write-Output "Disk space is okay."
}
```

Additional Notes

- **Multiple Comparisons:** You can chain comparisons together: 10 -lt $value -and $value -le 20 (Checks if $value is between 10 and 20).

- **Null Values:** Comparisons involving $null might give unexpected results, so be mindful.

Additional Resources

- **Microsoft Docs: About Comparison Operators:** https://docs.microsoft.com/en-us/powershell/module/microsoft.powershell.core/about/about_comparison_operators
- **Regular Expressions:** A powerful string-matching tool (We'll cover this later): https://en.wikipedia.org/wiki/Regular_expression

Practice Time

1. **Predictions:** Predict the output (True or False) of the following:
   - "HELLO" -eq "hello"
   - 100 -ge 50
   - 7 -lt 4
   - "Windows" -like "*dows"
2. **Script Tweaking:** Modify the disk space checking example to include a "critical" warning if the free space is less than 5 Gigabytes.

Up Next: More Comparisons

In Part 2 of "Comparison Operators," we'll look at additional comparison scenarios, type-specific operators, and how to combine comparisons for complex logic!

Comparison Operators, Part 2

In the previous chapter, we covered the core concepts of comparison operators. Now let's expand our toolbox and refine our ability to make precise comparisons in PowerShell.

Type-Specific Operators

PowerShell has operators designed to check for specific conditions related to data types:

- **-is, -isnot:** Checks if a value is of a specific type.
  - Example: `$value -is [string]`, `10 -isnot [bool]`
- **-as:** Attempts to cast a value to a specified type.
  - Example: `"123" -as [int]` (Successful if the string is a valid integer)

Working with Collections (Arrays, Hashtables)

- **-contains, -notcontains:** Checks if an item exists within an array or the keys of a hashtable.
  - Example: `1, 5, 10 -contains 5` (True)
- **-in, -notin:** The opposite of -contains and -notcontains (cleaner syntax for some). Example: `5 -in 1, 5, 10` (True)

Logical Operators: Combining Comparisons

To build more sophisticated conditions, use logical operators:

- **-and:** Both comparisons must be True for the result to be True.
- **-or:** At least one comparison must be True for the result to be True.
- **-not** (Negation): Reverses the result of an evaluation (e.g., `-not ($value -gt 10)`).

Example: Complex File Search

Let's imagine you need to find all files ending in `.log` that were modified in the last 24 hours:

```
$logFiles = Get-ChildItem -Filter "*.log"
$yesterdaysDate = (Get-Date).AddDays(-1)

$recentLogFiles = $logFiles | Where-Object {
    $_.LastWriteTime -gt $yesterdaysDate -and
$_.Name -like "*.log"
}
```

Explanation

1. We get all files with a .log extension.
2. We calculate yesterday's date.
3. Using `Where-Object`, we filter the `$logFiles` for those meeting both conditions: last modified after yesterday *and* the name ends in ".log".

Additional Considerations

- **Whitespace Sensitivity:** PowerShell can be picky about spaces around operators. Always ensure correct spacing (5 `-eq` 5 and not 5-eq5).
- **Precedence:** If you're unsure how multiple operators will be evaluated, use parentheses to enforce your intended order. Example: `($number -gt 5) -and ($number -lt 10)`.

Practice

1. **Type Exploration:** Write expressions using the `-is` and `-as` operators to test if different values are integers, strings, arrays, etc. Try to cast a string containing a number to an integer.
2. **Collection Checks:** Create a simple array of numbers. Use `-contains` (or `-in`) to check if a specific number exists in your array.
3. **Logical Challenge:** Build a script that takes user input for a username. Check if the input is NOT empty AND is longer than 5 characters.

Nesting Comparisons (Remember, this technique is not recommended)

While it's technically possible to nest comparisons directly (e.g., `1 -lt $value -lt 10`), this style can make your scripts hard to read. Using the `-and` operator is almost always clearer for combining multiple conditions.

Conclusion

By mastering comparison operators and the techniques in this chapter, you have the power to precisely control the flow of logic within your PowerShell scripts and start automating more complex decision-making tasks.

Coming Up... Cmdlets!

In the next chapter, we'll introduce cmdlets, the building blocks of PowerShell. Get ready to discover the pre-built commands that will give you superpowers over your system!

Introduction to Cmdlets

Forget about traditional command-line tools with their rigid syntax and limited output. Cmdlets are the heart and soul of PowerShell, designed to make your IT life significantly easier.

What are Cmdlets?

- **Pronounced:** "Command-lets"
- **Purpose:** Cmdlets are specialized built-in commands in PowerShell that perform specific actions. They follow a consistent `Verb-Noun` naming pattern, making them easy to discover and understand.
- **Output Objects:** Unlike traditional commands that often produce raw text, cmdlets output structured objects containing rich information that you can manipulate further down your PowerShell pipeline.

Examples of Common Cmdlets

- **Get-Service:** Gets a list of services on your system.
- **Get-Process:** Gets information about running processes.
- **Get-Help:** The most important cmdlet! Gets information about other cmdlets.
- **Stop-Process:** Stops a running process.
- **Set-Location:** Changes your current directory (like the `cd` command).

The Anatomy of a Cmdlet

Let's break down a typical cmdlet structure:

```
Get-Process -Name Explorer
```

- **Verb:** (`Get`) Indicates the type of action the cmdlet performs. Common verbs include Get, Set, Start, Stop, New, Remove.
- **Noun:** (`Process`) Specifies the resource the cmdlet acts upon.
- **Parameters:** (`-Name Explorer`) Optional modifiers that fine-tune the cmdlet's behavior (often starting with a dash '-')

PowerShell as a Toolkit

Think of PowerShell as a workshop and cmdlets as your specialized tools:

- **Get-ChildItem** is your flashlight for examining the contents of folders.
- **Where-Object** is your multi-purpose filter for selecting the exact objects you need.
- **Invoke-WebRequest** is your tool for interacting with websites.

Discovering Cmdlets

Let's use the powerful tools PowerShell gives you to explore its toolkit:

- **Get-Command:** The ultimate cmdlet finder!
  - `Get-Command *Service*` Lists cmdlets related to services.
  - `Get-Command -Verb Get` Shows all cmdlets with the "Get" verb.
- **Tab Completion:** Your best friend! As you type, press Tab to cycle through possible cmdlets and parameter names.

Help is Always Available

- **Get-Help -Examples:** Provides detailed help info and practical examples for a specific cmdlet. Try `Get-Help Get-Process -Examples`.
- **Get-Help -Online:** Opens the online documentation with even more comprehensive information.

Additional Resources

- **Microsoft's PowerShell Cmdlet Reference:**
  https://docs.microsoft.com/en-us/powershell/module/

Practice Time

1. **Exploration:** Use `Get-Command` to list cmdlets that have the following verbs:

- ○ Start
- ○ Stop
- ○ New

2. **Process Discovery:** Use `Get-Process` to see what's running on your system.
3. **Getting Help:** Run `Get-Help Get-Service -Examples` to learn more about the Get-Service cmdlet.

The Secret Sauce: Objects

Here's where PowerShell truly shines: Cmdlets don't just spit out text; they output structured objects that contain properties and methods. In the next chapters, you'll discover how to harness the power of these objects for sorting, filtering, and transforming data with unprecedented flexibility.

Up Next... Aliases

Ever found yourself wishing for shortcuts? Get ready to meet PowerShell aliases, those convenient nicknames for the cmdlets you'll be using frequently.

Leveraging Aliases

PowerShell understands that efficiency is key, especially when you're frequently using those long `Verb-Noun` cmdlets. Aliases offer a clever way to create custom shortcuts for your favorite (or frequently used) commands, making your PowerShell interactions faster and even a bit more fun!

What Are Aliases?

- **Nicknames for Cmdlets (and more)!** An alias is simply an alternative name that you can use to reference a cmdlet, function, script, or even an executable file.
- **Customization is Key:** PowerShell ships with many built-in aliases, but you also have the power to create your own.

Why Use Aliases?

1. **Speed:** Typing `ls` instead of `Get-ChildItem` saves precious keystrokes and gets things done quicker.
2. **Muscle Memory:** System admins coming from Linux/macOS feel more at home using familiar commands like `cd`, `ls`, and `clear`.
3. **Readability:** Sometimes a short alias can improve the readability of your scripts.
4. **Temporarily overriding commands:** If a cmdlet's name conflicts with something else, a temporary alias can be a solution.

Discovering Aliases

Use the `Get-Alias` cmdlet to see the aliases that are defined in your session:

- **Get-Alias** Lists all available aliases.
- **Get-Alias -Definition** Shows the alias associated with a specific cmdlet. Example: `Get-Alias -Definition Get-Process`

Common Built-in Aliases

PowerShell comes with a treasure chest of aliases for popular cmdlets:

Long Cmdlet	Alias(es)	Example Usage
Get-ChildItem	dir, ls, gci	`ls C:\Windows`
Where-Object	where, ?	`Get-Process | where {$_.mainWindowTitle -like "*Notepad*"}`
Select-Object	select	`Get-Service | select Name, Status`
ForEach-Object	foreach	`dir -recurse | foreach {$_.CreationTime}`

Creating Your Own Aliases

Use the `Set-Alias` cmdlet to unleash your shortcut creativity:

- **Basic Syntax:** `Set-Alias <alias-name> <command>`
  - Example: `Set-Alias restart Start-Service`
- **Scope:** By default, aliases you create only last for the current session. To make them permanent, you'll need to add them to your PowerShell profile (we'll cover this later).

Important Considerations

- **Choose Wisely:** Avoid alias names that might conflict with existing commands or that are too obscure to remember.
- **Don't Overdo It:** While aliases are handy, if you rely on them *too* heavily, it can make your scripts harder for others (or your future self) to understand.

The Power of Combining Aliases

Combine the use of aliases and your knowledge of cmdlets and parameters to execute commands in an efficient manner! For example, instead of writing this:

```
Get-ChildItem -Path C:\Windows -Filter *.txt
-Recurse
```

You could write this (assuming common aliases):

```
dir C:\Windows -file *.txt -s
```

Additional Resources

- **About Aliases (Microsoft Docs):**
  https://docs.microsoft.com/en-us/powershell/module/microsoft.powershell.core/about/about_aliases

Practice Time!

1. **Alias Hunt:** Use `Get-Alias` to list all the aliases available on your system. Spot any familiar ones from the Linux/macOS world?
2. **Make it Short:** Create aliases for the following cmdlets:
   - Get-Process
   - Stop-Process
   - Get-Help
3. **Customization:** If you come from a different command-line background, dig into `Get-Alias` and see if you can temporarily recreate some of your old favorite commands.

Next Up: PowerShell's Secret Weapon

Cmdlets are awesome, aliases make them faster, and in the next chapter, we'll unveil PowerShell's most powerful tool for finding the cmdlets and information you need - the mighty `Get-Help` system.

Finding Help and Resources

Even the most experienced PowerShell wizards sometimes need a helping hand. Knowing where to turn for reliable information is an essential skill for mastering PowerShell and solving problems efficiently. In this chapter, we'll arm you with tools and techniques to find the answers you need, ensuring your PowerShell journey is a smooth and productive one.

The Ultimate Command: Get-Help

PowerShell has an excellent built-in help system. `Get-Help` is your first line of defense and your gateway to understanding cmdlets:

- **Understanding Basics:** `Get-Help <cmdlet-name>` (e.g., `Get-Help Get-Service`) Displays basic syntax and parameter descriptions.
- **Detailed Help:** `Get-Help <cmdlet-name> -Detailed` Provides more in-depth information, including explanations for each parameter.
- **The Power of Examples:** `Get-Help <cmdlet-name> -Examples` Gives you practical usage scenarios, which are often the quickest way to understand how to apply a cmdlet.
- **Online Exploration:** `Get-Help <cmdlet-name> -Online` Takes you directly to the most up-to-date documentation on the Microsoft website.

Discovering New Commands

Often, you might know *what* you want to do, but not the *how*. Here's where `Get-Command` comes to the rescue:

- **Searching by Verb:** `Get-Command -Verb Start` Helps you find cmdlets related to starting things.
- **Searching by Noun:** `Get-Command -Noun Process` Lets you find cmdlets that deal with processes.
- **Wildcards:** `Get-Command -Noun *Service*` Utilizes wildcards for pattern-based searches.

Leveraging Tab Completion

Tab completion in PowerShell is your interactive best friend:

1. **Cmdlet Discovery:** Start typing a cmdlet name and press Tab to cycle through options that match what you've typed so far.
2. **Parameter Completion:** After typing a cmdlet, enter a space, a hyphen ('-'), and press Tab. PowerShell will cycle through available parameters for that cmdlet!

Mastering the Web: Resources

The internet is a treasure trove of PowerShell knowledge. Here are some key resources:

- **Microsoft's PowerShell Documentation:** https://docs.microsoft.com/en-us/powershell/ The official source with comprehensive cmdlet references and guides.
- **PowerShell Gallery:** https://www.powershellgallery.com/ A repository of community-created scripts, modules, and helpful resources.
- **TechNet and Stack Overflow:** Popular forums where you can search for solutions to common problems or ask your own questions.
- **PowerShell Blogs:** Many experts share tips, tricks, and advanced scripts through their blogs. A quick web search for "PowerShell Blogs" will yield a ton of resources.

Tips for Effective Searching

- **Be Specific:** The more specific your search terms, the better your results. Include cmdlet names, error messages, or the specific task you're trying to achieve.
- **Quotes Matter:** Use quotes to search for exact phrases, especially for error messages.
- **Leverage Examples:** Sometimes describing what you want to achieve through an example (e.g., "PowerShell get files older than a week") can lead you to the solution faster.

Learning from Others

- **Analyze Scripts:** The PowerShell Gallery, blogs, and forums often provide code snippets. Study them to understand how others approach problems and incorporate those techniques into your own scripts.
- **Don't Reinvent the Wheel:** Chances are, someone has likely already solved a problem similar to yours. Find and adapt existing solutions!

Practice

1. **Cmdlet Mystery:** Pick a cmdlet you're not familiar with. Use `Get-Help` (including `-Examples` and `-Online`) to learn its purpose and how to use it.
2. **Treasure Hunt:** Think of a task you'd like to automate in PowerShell, but you don't know the commands. Use web searches, forums, or the PowerShell Gallery to find how others might have tackled this.

Conclusion

By mastering the tools and resources covered in this chapter, you'll unlock a wealth of PowerShell knowledge. Remember, finding answers efficiently is a crucial skill in your PowerShell journey.

Next: Unleashing the Power of Objects

In the next chapter, we'll start our exploration of PowerShell's object-oriented magic and how it revolutionizes the way we work with data.

Section 2:
Object Manipulation in PowerShell

Introduction to Objects

If you've used other scripting or command-line environments, you're likely accustomed to working with raw text. PowerShell takes a revolutionary leap forward by making *objects* the first-class citizens of its universe.

What is an Object?

- **Digital Entities:** Objects are like digital representations of real-world things or concepts. A file, a running process, a network printer – these can all be modeled as objects in PowerShell.
- **Bundles of Data and Functionality:** An object has two core components:
  - **Properties:** Characteristics that describe the object. A file object has properties like Name, Size, CreationTime, etc.
  - **Methods:** Actions you can perform on the object. A file object might have methods to Copy, Move, or Delete itself.

Why Objects Matter

1. **Structured Data** Unlike the flat textual output of traditional commands, objects provide a rich, structured way to represent and interact with information.
2. **Discoverability:** Objects are self-documenting. By examining an object's properties and methods, you gain a deeper understanding of what you can do with it.
3. **The Pipeline Powerhouse:** PowerShell's true magic comes alive when you chain cmdlets together in a pipeline, passing objects between them for seamless filtering, sorting, and transformation.

A Simple Example

Let's get a feel for objects. Run the following command in your PowerShell console:

```
Get-Process -Name notepad
```

This outputs something like this (simplified for brevity):

Handles	NPM(K)	PM(K)	WS(K)	CPU(s)	Id	SI	ProcessName
368	12	3084	14872	0.13	8192	1	notepad

- **It's Not Just Text:** While this looks like a neatly formatted table, PowerShell sees this differently.
- **A Process Object:** Each row represents a single process object, with properties such as:
  - Handles
  - NPM(K) (Non-paged Memory)
  - Id (Process Id)
  - ProcessName

Unlocking Object Secrets: Get-Member

The Get-Member cmdlet is your key to exploring the structure of objects:

1. **Pipe into Get-Member:** Get-Process -Name notepad | Get-Member
2. **Dissecting the Object:** You'll see a listing of:
   - **MemberType:** Identifies if it's a Property, Method, etc.
   - **Name:** The name of the property or method.

Using Object Properties

Let's get practical:

```
$notepad = Get-Process -Name notepad  # Store the object
$notepad.StartTime   # Access the StartTime Property
```

Methods in Action

```
$service = Get-Service -Name spooler # Get the Print
Spooler service
$service.Stop()                        # Call the
Stop() method
```

Additional Resources

- **About Objects (Microsoft Docs):**
  https://docs.microsoft.com/en-us/powershell/module/microsoft.powershell.core/about/about_objects

Let's Get Practical

1. **Object Exploration:**
   - Use `Get-Service` to retrieve a service object (any service on your system). Pipe it into `Get-Member`. Examine the properties and methods.
2. **Process Property Fun:**
   - Access the `Path` property of a running process (like Notepad or a browser) to find where its executable is located.

Up Next: Sorting and Organizing

Now that you understand the fundamentals of objects, we're ready to harness their power! Next, we'll learn how to sort, group, and arrange objects in PowerShell, enabling you to slice and dice data with incredible flexibility.

Sorting and Organizing Data

The ability to arrange and structure data is essential for extracting meaningful insights. In PowerShell, when you're working with collections of objects, you have powerful tools at your fingertips to sort them by specific properties, group them together, and present the information in the most useful way.

Sorting with Sort-Object

The `Sort-Object` cmdlet is your go-to command for ordering PowerShell objects.

1. **Basic Sorting:**

   ```
   Get-Process | Sort-Object -Property WorkingSet #
   Sort by memory usage
   ```

2. **Descending Order:** Add the `-Descending` parameter to reverse the sort order.

   ```
   Get-Service | Sort-Object Status -Descending #
   Running services first
   ```

3. **Multiple Properties:** Sort by several criteria:

   ```
   Get-ChildItem | Sort-Object Length, Name # Sort
   by size, then file name
   ```

Example: Analyzing Disk Space

Let's imagine you need a list of the largest files in a directory:

```
Get-ChildItem -Path C:\Windows -Recurse |
    Sort-Object Length -Descending |
    Select-Object Name, Directory, Length -First 10
```

Explanation

1. `Get-ChildItem -Recurse` gets all files within the Windows folder and its subfolders.

2. `Sort-Object Length -Descending` sorts files by their size with the largest first.
3. `Select-Object -First 10` picks only the top 10 results.

Grouping Data with Group-Object

Sometimes sorting isn't enough—you need to categorize objects based on a shared characteristic. That's where `Group-Object` shines.

- **Grouping Principle:** `Group-Object` takes an input collection and creates groups where the objects within each group have the same value in a specified property.

Example: Services Grouped by Status

```
Get-Service | Group-Object Status
```

Output(simplified)

```
Count Name              Group
----- ----              -----
   60 Stopped           {Service1, Service5, Service12, ...}
   32 Running           {Service2, Service8, ...}
```

Now you can easily analyze how many services are running vs. stopped.

Advanced Use Cases

- **Calculating Group Metrics** (e.g., total file size per file extension, number of processes per user)
- **Creating Custom Views** For reporting or data visualization

Additional Resources

- **Sort-Object Documentation:** https://docs.microsoft.com/en-us/powershell/module/microsoft.powershell.utility/sort-object
- **Group-Object Documentation:** https://docs.microsoft.com/en-us/powershell/module/microsoft.powershell.utility/group-object

Practice Time!

1. **Biggest Memory Hogs:** Use `Get-Process`, `Sort-Object`, and `Select-Object` to display the top 5 processes on your system consuming the most working set memory.
2. **File Extensions Breakdown:** Use `Get-ChildItem` and `Group-Object` to get a count of the different file extensions present in a directory of your choice.

Customization: Calculated Properties

Sometimes you might need to sort or group based on data that's not directly present as a property. Calculated properties let you generate new values on the fly using expressions. See Microsoft's documentation for details!

Next Up: Filtering with Where-Object

We've covered sorting and organizing. Now get ready to master the `Where-Object` cmdlet, which will empower you to pinpoint specific objects using PowerShell's flexible filtering logic.

Filtering with the `Where-Object` Cmdlet

Think of the `Where-Object` cmdlet as your intelligent detective within the PowerShell pipeline. It meticulously examines the objects flowing through and allows only those that match your specific criteria to pass. This is how you'll pinpoint the exact data you need to solve your IT automation challenges.

The Basics of Filtering

The core structure of `Where-Object` follows this pattern:

```
Get-Something | Where-Object { $_.<Property>
-<comparison operator> <value> }
```

Let's break it down:

- **Get-Something:** Start with a cmdlet that produces a collection of objects.
- **Where-Object:** Begins the filtering process.
- **{ ... }:** This is a Script Block – a piece of PowerShell code where your filtering logic resides.
- **$_:** Represents the current object being evaluated within the script block.
- **.:** The name of the object property you want to compare.
- **- Like -eq, -lt, -gt, -like, etc. (We covered these in the Comparison Operators chapter).
- **:** The value you're comparing the property against.

Example: Find Old Files

```
Get-ChildItem -Path C:\Temp | Where-Object
{$_.LastWriteTime -lt (Get-Date).AddDays(-7) }
```

This finds files in "C:\Temp" that haven't been modified in the last 7 days.

More Filtering Power

- **Multiple Conditions:** Combine conditions using logical operators (`-and`, `-or`). Example: Files larger than 10 MB AND with a .log extension:

```
... Where-Object {$_.Length -gt 10MB -and
$_.Extension -eq ".log" }
```

- **String Matching:** `-like` (wildcard matching) and `-match` (regular expressions) give you flexible ways to filter text.

Real-World Scenarios

1. **Stale Service Hunting:** Find services that haven't been started recently:

```
Get-Service | Where-Object { $_.Status -eq
"Stopped" -and $_.StartTime -lt
(Get-Date).AddDays(-30) }
```

2. **Process by Owner:** Get processes owned by a specific user:

```
Get-Process | Where-Object {
$_.StartInfo.UserName -eq "jane.doe" }
```

Additional Notes

- **Aliases:** `Where-Object` can be shortened to 'where' or its symbol alias '?'
- **Performance:** For large collections of objects, filtering earlier in the pipeline is generally more efficient.

Additional Resources

- **Regular Expressions for the uninitiated:**
  https://en.wikipedia.org/wiki/Regular_expression

Practice Time!

1. **Critical Processes:** List processes where the CPU usage is consistently above 90% (requires monitoring for a short period—hint: you might need to collect several samples).
2. **Disk Space Offenders:** In a directory of your choice, find image files (.jpg, .png, etc.) that exceed a size of 2 MB.

Pro Tip: Combining Filtering & Formatting

The objects that pass through `Where-Object` can be further formatted or customized using cmdlets like `Select-Object` or `Format-Table`. This allows you to refine the final output. (We'll cover formatting in an upcoming chapter)

Next: Mastering Loops for Powerful Automation

Filtering empowers you to select objects. Now let's get ready to unleash automation superpowers using PowerShell's looping constructs, enabling you to perform actions repeatedly over entire sets of data with breathtaking efficiency!

Using Loops for Filtering

Sometimes your filtering logic can't be expressed in a single `Where-Object` statement. Loops provide the flexibility to apply more complex, multi-step analysis to sets of objects—giving you custom, fine-grained control over how data is filtered within your PowerShell scripts.

Introducing Loops

Before we dive into combining with filtering, let's get the basics of loops:

- **Iteration:** Loops fundamentally repeat a block of code multiple times.
- **Common Loop Types:**
  - `for` loop: Iterates a set number of times based on a counter.
  - `foreach` loop: Iterates over every item in a collection (most common with objects).
  - `while` loop: Repeats as long as a specific condition is true.
  - `do-while`/`do-until`: Variants of the 'while' loop.

Filtering Within Loops

Here's the general pattern of how you'd use a loop to perform advanced filtering:

1. **Get Objects:** Start with a cmdlet that outputs your initial collection of objects.
2. **Loop:** Use a `for`, `foreach`, or `while` loop to process each object individually.
3. **Conditional Logic:** Within the loop's code block, use `if` statements to apply your filtering criteria.
4. **Action:** Take actions based on the results of the filtering. This might involve collecting the objects that match, modifying them, or triggering other commands.

Example: Filtering Files with Complex Criteria

Let's say you need to find all files that meet ALL of the following:

- Located under 'C:\Reports'
- File extension is '.pdf'.
- Larger than 500 KB
- Haven't been accessed in the past 60 days.

Here's how you could achieve this using a `foreach` loop:

```
$reportFiles = Get-ChildItem -Path C:\Reports
-Filter *.pdf

foreach ($file in $reportFiles) {
    if ($file.Length -gt 500KB -and
$file.LastAccessTime -lt (Get-Date).AddDays(-60)) {
        # File matches! Take Action:
        $file.FullName  # Could display the path,
move the file, or perform another operation
    }
}
```

Why Use Loops for Filtering?

- **Complex Conditions:** When `Where-Object` alone isn't expressive enough, loops provide granular control over your filtering logic.
- **Custom Actions:** Within the loop, you can perform actions beyond simply selecting or rejecting objects. This opens up scenarios like modifying the matching objects or using the filtered data to trigger external processes.

Performance Note

For simple filtering, `Where-Object` is usually most efficient. When you need sophisticated logic or custom actions, loops become essential.

Practice Makes Perfect

1. **Recent Large Temp Files:** Write a script that uses a loop to find files in your temporary directory (you can find this using environment variables), filtering them based on these criteria:
   - Created in the last 24 hours.

- Size exceeds 10 MB

2. **Advanced Process Filter:** Create a script that lists processes taking up significant memory and meets one or more of the following:
   - Process Name doesn't start with "svchost"
   - CPU time higher than 30 seconds.

Next Up: Mastering the 'Foreach' Loop

The foreach loop is a natural partner for object manipulation tasks in PowerShell. In the next chapter, we'll take a deep dive into its capabilities and the common patterns you'll employ in your scripts.

Mastering Foreach **Loops: Part 1**

The foreach loop is your go-to tool for iterating over collections of objects in PowerShell. Its elegance lies in how naturally it handles the pipeline, letting you process objects one by one and perform a huge range of actions.

Basic Foreach Loop Structure

```
foreach ($item in $collection) {
    # Code to execute for each $item
}
```

Let's dissect this:

- **$collection:** This is the collection of items you want to loop through (e.g., an array, output from a cmdlet, etc.)
- **$item:** A variable name that will represent the current object during each iteration of the loop.
- **Code Block:** The code inside the curly braces { } will be executed for every object in the collection.

Example: Analyzing Processes

```
foreach ($process in Get-Process) {
    "Process: $($process.Name) - Memory:
$($process.WorkingSet / 1MB) MB"
}
```

How it Works

1. Get-Process outputs a collection of process objects.
2. Foreach takes the first object and assigns it to the $process variable.
3. The code block executes, displaying process information.
4. Foreach moves to the next process object, and the loop repeats until all objects have been processed.

PowerShell's Secret: The Pipeline

`Foreach` often works with cmdlets that produce a collection of objects. Consider this:

```
Get-Service | foreach { $_.Name + " - " + $_.Status}
```

The output from `Get-Service` is piped directly into the `foreach` loop, seamlessly providing the collection to iterate over!

Common Use Cases

- **Property Access:** Easily display or manipulate specific properties of each object in the collection.
- **Filtering Inside the Loop** Use `if` statements within the loop for more nuanced selection (as we saw in the previous chapter).
- **Transforming Objects:** Modify or calculate new values based on each object's data.
- **External Actions:** Interact with systems outside of PowerShell, passing data from the loop to other commands, scripts, or even web APIs.

The $_ Placeholder: Your Friend

Remember, `$_` inside the `foreach` code block represents the current object. This makes accessing properties wonderfully simple.

Additional Resources

- **About_Foreach:**
  https://docs.microsoft.com/en-us/powershell/module/microsoft.powershell.core/about/about_foreach

Practice Time

1. **File Details:** Write a script using `Get-ChildItem` and `foreach` to display the following for each file in a directory:
   - Name
   - Size in KB
   - Creation Date
2. **Selective Service Commands:** Use `Get-Service` and a `foreach` loop. Inside the loop, add an `if` condition to check if the

service status is "Running". If it is, stop the service using
`Stop-Service`.

Part 2: More Power Techniques

In the next chapter, we'll delve into controlling loop flow, alternative syntax like the `ForEach-Object` cmdlet, and how these loops make transforming data a breeze!

Mastering Foreach Loops: Part 2

In the previous chapter, we laid the foundation for the foreach loop. Now it's time to level up your skills with control flow, alternative forms, and object transformation techniques.

Controlling Flow Within the Loop

- **break:** Use the break keyword to immediately exit the foreach loop, often based on a specific condition.
- **continue:** The continue keyword skips the current iteration and jumps to the next item in the collection.

Example: Processing with Exceptions

```
foreach ($file in Get-ChildItem -Path C:\temp) {
    if ($file.Length -gt 500MB) {
        Write-Warning "$($file.Name) is very large!"
        continue  # Skip further processing for this
file
    }
    # Additional processing for smaller files
}
```

ForEach-Object – Another Flavor of Foreach

PowerShell offers ForEach-Object (alias '%') as a more pipeline-centric alternative to the traditional foreach statement.

Key Differences:

- **Syntax:** Focused on piping objects into it
- **Performance:** Can sometimes be optimized by the PowerShell engine

Example:

```
Get-Service | ForEach-Object {
    "Service: $($_.Name) - Status: $($_.Status)"
```

```
}
```

Transformation Power

Foreach loops excel at transforming objects as they pass through. Let's look at a common pattern:

```
$services = Get-Service | foreach {
    # Creating a custom object
    [PSCustomObject]@{
        Name = $_.Name
        Status = $_.Status
        CanStop = $_.CanStop
    }
}
```

Explanation

1. We get services using Get-Service.
2. For every service object, we construct a new [PSCustomObject] on the fly.
3. We populate properties ('Name', 'Status', 'CanStop') with selective data from the original service object.
4. The result, $services, is a new collection of our custom-designed objects.

Additional Resources

- **About Break:**
  https://docs.microsoft.com/en-us/powershell/module/microsoft.powershell.core/about/about_break
- **About Continue:**
  https://docs.microsoft.com/en-us/powershell/module/microsoft.powershell.core/about/about_continue

Practice

1. **Counting File Types:** Use a foreach loop, and group file extensions in a directory. Output a count of how many files you have of each type (e.g., 30 JPG files, 10 DOCX files, etc.). (Hint:

You might find the concept of a hash table useful - we'll cover those soon!)

2. **Custom Process Table:** Get process information using `Get-Process`. Within a `foreach` loop, create custom objects containing the following:
   - Process Name
   - CPU Usage (you may need to sample this over a few seconds)
   - Whether the process has a main window (`.MainWindowTitle`)

Key Takeaways

- Control loop behavior precisely using `break` and `continue`.
- `ForEach-Object` provides a pipeline-friendly way to iterate.
- Use `foreach` to transform collections of objects, designing the output structure you need.

Coming Up Next: Arrays!

Arrays are fundamental for storing ordered lists of items. Next, we'll learn how to create, manipulate, and work with arrays in PowerShell, opening up a whole new world of data processing possibilities!

Working with Arrays: Part 1

Arrays are essential data structures in any programming language, and PowerShell is no exception. They provide a structured way to store and manage collections of items under a single variable name. If you've used arrays in other languages, the concepts will be familiar with a PowerShell twist!

What is an Array?

- **Ordered Collection:** An array stores multiple items in a specific sequence.
- **Indexing:** You access individual elements of an array using their index (numerical position), starting from zero.

Creating Arrays

There are several ways to create arrays in PowerShell:

1. **Comma-Separated Values:**

   ```
   $numbers = 1, 2, 5, 10
   ```

2. **Array Operator '()':** For more control and mixing data types:

   ```
   $mixedArray = @(10, "hello", $true, Get-Date)
   ```

3. **Empty Array + Assignment:** Create an empty array, then add items

   ```
   $fileNames = @()
   $fileNames += "report.txt"
   $fileNames += "data.csv"
   ```

Accessing and Modifying Elements

Use square brackets [ ] with the element's index:

```
$numbers = 1, 5, 8, 12
$numbers[0]      # Accesses the first element (1)
```

```
$numbers[2] = 99 # Modifies the third element
```

Key Properties and Methods

- **.Count:** Returns the number of elements in an array.

  ```
  $numbers.Count
  ```

- **.Length:** (Synonym for .Count)

Common Array Operations

- **Adding Items:** Use the + operator (creates a new array)

  ```
  $newArray = $numbers + 20
  ```

- **Removing Specific Elements:** This is trickier than other languages. See the following resources for techniques.

Iterating over Arrays

Foreach is your best friend for working with elements in an array:

```
$services = "DHCP", "DNS", "Print Spooler"
foreach ($service in $services) {
    Write-Output "Starting service: $service"
    Start-Service $service
}
```

Additional Resources

- **About Arrays:**
  https://docs.microsoft.com/en-us/powershell/module/microsoft.powershell.core/about/about_arrays

Practice

1. **Number Calculations:**
   - Create an array with the numbers 10 through 20.
   - Use a loop to calculate the sum and average of the numbers.
2. **Task List:**
   - Create an array of daily tasks (strings).

    ○ Iterate over the tasks, displaying them with an index number to give a numbered task list.

Why Arrays Matter

- **Structured Data:** Arrays bring order when working with multiple items.
- **Automation:** Loops and arrays are a powerful combination for automating tasks that involve lists or sequences.

Next: More Array Power

In Part 2, we'll dive into more advanced array manipulation techniques, including searching, filtering, and advanced array creation methods!

Working with Arrays: Part 2

Let's build upon your array skills! In this chapter, we'll explore techniques that give you even more control over this versatile data structure.

Searching Within Arrays

Often you'll need to locate specific elements within an array:

- **Index Of:** The `[array].IndexOf()` method tells you the index of the first occurrence of a value.

```
$numbers = 5, 12, 9, 3, 9
$numbers.IndexOf(9)   # Outputs: 2
```

- **Contains:** Use the `-contains` operator to check if a value exists at all:

```
$services = "DNS", "Print Spooler"
$services -contains "DHCP"  # Outputs: False
```

Filtering Arrays

Let's use our PowerShell object-smarts to filter arrays:

1. **Using Where-Object:**

```
$processes = Get-Process
$largeProcesses = $processes | Where-Object
{$_.WorkingSet -gt 500MB}
```

2. **Advanced Script Block Filtering:** Filter on multiple criteria or complex logic within the `Where-Object` script block.

Sorting Arrays

The `Sort-Object` cmdlet comes in handy for arrays too!

```
$folders = Get-ChildItem -Directory
$folders | Sort-Object CreationTime -Descending  #
Sorts by newest first
```

Advanced Array Creation

Beyond the basics, PowerShell offers some neat ways to build arrays:

- **Range Operator:** Create an array of numbers in a sequence.

  ```
  $numbers = 1..10  # Creates an array [1, 2, 3,
  ... 10]
  ```

- **The '..' Operator with ForEach-Object:**

  ```
  $squares = 1..5 | ForEach-Object { $_ * $_ }
  $squares  # Contains [1, 4, 9, 16, 25]
  ```

Multidimensional Arrays

While less common, you can create arrays within arrays for complex data structures. See Microsoft's documentation for details.

Important: Arrays vs. Output Collections

Often what looks like an array in PowerShell output is not a "true" array. Some cmdlets output collections that may need special handling. Let's see an example:

```
$processes = Get-Process
$processes.Name  # Looks like an array, but might
not be!
```

Practice Time

1. **Process Filtering:**
   - Get a list of running processes.
   - Find the index of the first process named "explorer" if it exists.
   - Create a new array that only contains processes consuming more than 100 MB of working set memory.

2. **File Management:**
   - Get all files in a directory.
   - Create a new array that only contains the names of the ".log" files.
   - Sort the file names alphabetically.

Key Points

- Arrays are not just lists – they offer searching, filtering, and sorting power.
- Distinguish between true arrays and cmdlet output that appears like an array.

Coming Up: Hash Tables

Next, we'll introduce hash tables – a powerful way to store data using key-value pairs, offering fast lookups and flexibility that arrays can't always match.

Using Hash Tables for Data Organization

If arrays are like ordered lists, hash tables are like super-powered dictionaries. They let you associate values with custom keys, enabling quick lookups and offering a structured way to represent complex information.

What is a Hash Table?

- **Key-Value Pairs:** The fundamental building block. A "key" is like a unique label, and it's associated with a "value".
- **Also known as:** Hash tables are sometimes called associative arrays or dictionaries in other languages.
- **Structure:** Enclosed in curly braces @{ }, key-value pairs are separated by semicolons.

Creating Hash Tables

```
$processInfo = @{
    Name = "chrome.exe"
    Id = 1234
    StartTime = (Get-Date)
}
```

Accessing and Modifying Values

- **By Key:** Similar to object property access:

```
$processInfo.Name  # Outputs "chrome.exe"
$processInfo.Id = 5678  # Modifies the value
```

- **Adding New Pairs:**

```
$processInfo.Path = "C:\Program
Files\Chrome.exe"
```

Why Use Hash Tables?

1. **Fast Lookups:** Retrieving a value by its key is extremely efficient, unlike searching through arrays.
2. **Flexibility:** Keys and values can be almost any data type (numbers, strings, objects, even arrays!). Perfect for modeling real-world data structures.
3. **Readability:** The key-value format makes code more intuitive and easier to understand.

Example: Representing a File

```
$fileInfo = @{
    Name = "report.pdf"
    Size = 256000   # In bytes
    CreationTime = (Get-Date).AddDays(-5)
    Attributes = "Archive"
}
```

Iterating over Hash Tables

Use Foreach to work with key-value pairs:

```
foreach ($key in $processInfo.Keys) {
    "$key: $($processInfo.$key)"
}
```

Additional Resources

- **About Hash Tables:**
  https://docs.microsoft.com/en-us/powershell/module/microsoft.powershell.core/about/about_hash_tables

Practice

1. **Service Status Lookup:**
   o Create a hash table where the keys are service names and the values are their statuses ("Running", "Stopped").
   o Write a snippet to get the status of a service given its name.
2. **Task Tracker:**
   o Create a hash table to represent a task:
     ■ Name (string)

- DueDate (DateTime Object)
- Completed (True/False)
  - Create a few tasks and practice adding or modifying them using their keys.

Hash Tables in Action

Hash tables shine in real-world scenarios like:

- **Configuration Data:** Store settings loaded from files or user input.
- **Web API Interaction:** Parsing JSON often results in hash table-like structures.
- **Grouping Objects:** You can use hash tables with `Group-Object` for advanced grouping scenarios.

Up Next: Formatting and Output

We've covered powerful data structures! Now let's explore how to format and present this data in user-friendly and customized ways – essential for reports, dashboards, or even simple console output.

Section 3:
Handling, Storing, and Importing Data

Output Formatting Basics

So far, much of our PowerShell interaction has been on the console. While functional, the default output often leaves a lot to be desired for readability and professional presentation. In this chapter, we'll learn the fundamentals of formatting and how to gain control over the data you display.

Understanding Default Formatting

PowerShell has built-in rules for how it displays different objects. You've likely seen these:

- **Processes:** Get-Process usually outputs a table-like view.
- **Services:** Get-Service also produces a table.
- **Files:** Get-ChildItem gives you a basic directory listing.

Behind the Scenes

PowerShell's formatting system is surprisingly complex! Here's a simplified explanation:

1. **Object Types Matter:** Objects have hidden type information that PowerShell uses.
2. **Format Files:** PowerShell has .format.ps1xml files that define how to display certain types of objects. You can even create your own!

The Three Core Formatting Cmdlets

Let's introduce the primary tools you'll use:

- **Format-List (alias: fl)**: Displays objects as a list of properties and their values.
  - Example: `Get-Service | Format-List *` (shows all properties)
- **Format-Table (alias: ft)**: The classic tabular view. Choose which properties to include as columns.
  - Example: `Get-Process | Format-Table Name, WorkingSet`
- **Format-Wide (alias: fw)**: Best for displaying only a single property of a wider object.
  - Example: `Get-ChildItem | Format-Wide Name`

Key Points

- **Formatting Doesn't Change the Objects:** PowerShell's object magic remains. Formatting only affects how the objects are displayed.
- **Pipeline Power:** Formatting cmdlets are usually placed at the end of your pipeline to shape the final output.

Taking Control: Selecting Properties

Often you only want a subset of an object's properties. Let's format a service:

```
Get-Service -Name spooler | Format-List Name,
Status, DisplayName
```

Output to Other Cmdlets

Instead of going to the console, formatting cmdlets can also feed other tools:

- **Out-GridView:** Interactive, searchable, and filterable table.
- **Export-Csv:** Converts objects into CSV files (perfect for spreadsheets or data processing). We'll cover files in the next chapter!

Additional Resources

- **Help on Formatting Cmdlets:**
    - `Get-Help Format-Table -Online`
    - `Get-Help Format-List -Online`
    - ...and more!
- **The 'Out' Cmdlets:'** `Get-Help Out-*`

Practice

1. **Custom Process View:** Use `Get-Process`, select the following properties and display them as a table:
    - Id
    - ProcessName
    - CPU (you might need to calculate this briefly)
2. **Formatted File Listing:** Get files in a directory and use `Format-Wide` to display only their names and last modified dates.

What's Next?

Basic formatting is a start, but PowerShell allows for much more! In the next chapter, we'll learn advanced formatting techniques to create tailored and polished output.

Advanced Output Formatting

Let's move beyond basic formatting and dive into how PowerShell lets you achieve precisely customized and informative output. In the previous chapter, we laid the foundation. Now, it's time to unleash your formatting creativity! We'll explore techniques for calculated properties, creating table layouts, and even a touch of HTML output.

Calculated Properties

Sometimes you need to display data that isn't directly in an object's properties. Enter calculated properties, created directly in your `Format-*` cmdlets:

```
Get-Process | Format-Table Name, WorkingSet,
@{Name="WS(MB)"; Expression = {$_.WorkingSet / 1MB}}
```

Explanation

1. **@{ ... }**: This defines a calculated property.
2. **Name:** The name of your new column.
3. **Expression:** A script block where $_ represents the current object.

Formatting Filesystem Objects

Let's make file listings more useful. Calculate file size in KB:

```
Get-ChildItem | Format-Table Name, Length,
@{Name="Size(KB)";Expression={$_.Length / 1KB}}
```

Customizing Tables

You can fine-tune how tables are displayed:

- **AutoSize:** Have columns adjust their width based on content. Add this to `Format-Table`.
- **Wrap:** For long text properties, force them to wrap within cells (also for `Format-Table`).

Example: Nicer Service View

```
Get-Service | Format-Table -AutoSize Name, Status,
Description -Wrap
```

Output as HTML

The `ConvertTo-Html` cmdlet can turn PowerShell objects into basic HTML fragments. This is useful for simple reports or web displays:

```
Get-Process | Where-Object {$_.CPU -gt 10} |
    Select Name, Description |
    ConvertTo-Html -Fragment -Title "High CPU
Processes"
```

Note: HTML output is basic, styling will likely need further refinement if this is for a web interface.

Advanced Concepts (a brief mention)

- **Custom Format Files:** You can define your own `.format.ps1xml` files to achieve extremely precise control over object display. This is a complex topic, so we'll just introduce it here. See Microsoft docs for more.
- **Formatting for Different Purposes:** The best formatting approach depends on whether the output is for the console, a log file, a CSV for spreadsheets, or something else entirely!

Additional Resources

- **ConvertTo-Html:** https://docs.microsoft.com/en-us/powershell/module/microsoft.powershell.utility/convertto-html

Practice

1. **Enhanced Network Stats:** Get network adapter information using `Get-NetAdapter`. Create a table view that includes:
   - Name
   - Status
   - MAC Address

    ○ Speed (calculated, careful with units!)

2. **HTML Process Report:** Create a basic HTML report of the top 5 processes by memory usage. Include their name, memory (in MB), and a short description.

Key Takeaways

- Calculated properties let you output information not directly contained within a basic object.
- Consider your output's target audience when adjusting table formatting.
- PowerShell can even give you simple HTML output for basic reporting.

Coming Up: Storing Data

We've mastered formatting. Next, we'll tackle how to store and persist the data you've so beautifully formatted – from files (like CSVs and JSON) to interacting with external databases!

Saving Data to Files – Part 1

Outputting to the console is fleeting. Often, you need to persist the results of your PowerShell work. This chapter will introduce core concepts and cmdlets to turn your objects into structured data within files.

Why Save Data to Files?

- **Persistence:** Data in files survives beyond your current PowerShell session.
- **Transfer and Exchange:** Files are a universal way to share data between systems, tools, or people.
- **Analysis:** External tools like Excel can work with data stored within files.
- **Automation Archives:** Create records or logs of your script's actions.

CSV (Comma-Separated Values)

One of the most common and versatile formats:

- **Simple Structure:** Rows of data, with values separated by commas.
- **Tool Friendly:** Easily consumed by spreadsheets, databases, and other software.

Exporting to CSV with Export-Csv

Let's save a list of processes as a CSV:

```
Get-Process | Export-Csv -Path processes.csv
-NoTypeInformation
```

- **-NoTypeInformation:** Often useful to remove PowerShell-specific object details.

Key Points About CSV

- **First Line is Header:** The first row usually defines the column names.

- **Handling Complex Data:** If your objects have nested properties, it may take some extra work (`Select-Object`) to get a clean CSV.

Out-File: The Basics

`Out-File` offers a basic way to send text to a file.

```
Get-Date | Out-File -FilePath current_date.txt
```

- **Overwrites By Default:** Use `-Append` to add to an existing file.
- **Formatting Note:** `Out-File` generally works best with pre-formatted strings, not rich objects.

Custom Text Formatting

Building your own output lets you structure data exactly as needed:

```
foreach ($service in Get-Service) {
    "$($service.Name), $($service.Status)" |
Out-File -Append services.txt
}
```

Additional Resources

- **All About Export-Csv:**
  https://docs.microsoft.com/en-us/powershell/module/microsoft.powershell.utility/export-csv
- **Out-File In Detail:**
  https://docs.microsoft.com/en-us/powershell/module/microsoft.powershell.utility/out-file

Practice Time

1. **File System Report**
   - Use `Get-ChildItem` in a specific directory.
   - Export a CSV containing: Name, Creation Time, Last Modified Time, Size (in KB), Full Path
2. **Advanced Process Log:**
   - Get running processes, but include start time, process owner, and path.

- ○ Build your own custom formatted text file where each process is on its own line, neatly organized with columns.

Up Next: JSON and Advanced Techniques

Simple file saves are just the beginning! In the next chapter, we'll cover JSON (a powerful data exchange format) and some more specialized export techniques that PowerShell offers.

Saving Data to Files – Part 2

Let's expand your file-saving toolkit! In this chapter, we'll cover JSON, a powerful format for structured data, and some specialized techniques for less common scenarios.

JSON (JavaScript Object Notation)

- **Hierarchical Data:** JSON supports nested objects, arrays – great for representing complex data structures.
- **Web Standard:** Widely used for exchanging data with web services.
- **Human Readable:** Compared to formats like XML, JSON can be easier for humans to understand.

ConvertTo-Json and Out-File

PowerShell makes working with JSON easy:

```
$services = Get-Service | Select-Object Name,
Status, StartType
```

```
$services | ConvertTo-Json | Out-File services.json
```

Important: `ConvertTo-Json` has a `-Depth` parameter to control how many levels of nesting are included. Experiment!

XML (Extensible Markup Language)

While less common these days, you might encounter it:

- **More Structured Than CSV:** XML uses tags to define data elements.
- **Legacy Systems:** Some older systems or data formats may use XML.

Saving as XML

```
Get-Process | Export-Clixml processes.xml
```

Note: `Export-CliXml` is PowerShell's tool for creating XML files.

Beyond the Basics

Let's look at some less common, but useful techniques for saving data:

1. **Appending to Files:** Both `Out-File` and `Export-Csv` have an `-Append` parameter to add data to the end of an existing file.
2. **Encoding:** For text files, consider the `-Encoding` parameter (available on many file-related cmdlets). Examples: 'UTF8', 'ASCII'.
3. **Binary Data:** PowerShell can work with files containing raw bytes. See the `Set-Content` cmdlet with its `-Encoding Byte` option.

Additional Resources

- **JSON in PowerShell:**
  https://docs.microsoft.com/en-us/powershell/module/microsoft.powershell.utility/convertto-json

Practice

1. **Enhanced Process JSON:**
   - Get process information, including process owners.
   - Use `ConvertTo-Json` and save as a .json file. Experiment with `-Depth` to find a good balance of detail.
2. **Investigate XML:** If you have a system or tool that produces XML, use PowerShell's `Get-Content` to load it and examine the structure. Hint: PowerShell treats well-formed XML as objects!

Key Considerations

- **File Format Choice:** CSV for simple tables, JSON for richer data, XML only if necessary.
- **Data Complexity:** The more complex your objects, the trickier getting a perfect CSV might be.

What's Next? Importing Data!

Now that you can save data, the next logical step is learning to read it back in! We'll cover importing from CSVs, JSON, and other sources, allowing you to build data-driven PowerShell workflows.

Importing Data from Various Sources

Let's dive into the world of importing data into PowerShell. Data is power, and this chapter will equip you to bring in external information to fuel your scripts and automation! We've learned how to produce data using cmdlets and save it to files. The complementary skill is reading data *in*, empowering your scripts to process information from the outside world.

CSV (Comma-Separated Values)

Let's begin with one of the most universal data-exchange formats:

- **Import-Csv to the Rescue:** The `Import-Csv` cmdlet is your primary tool for loading CSVs into PowerShell.

  ```
  $processList = Import-Csv -Path processes.csv
  ```

- **Result: Objects!** PowerShell generally turns each row into an object, properties matching the CSV's header columns.

Key Points About CSV Import

- **Delimiter:** If your CSV uses something other than commas (e.g., tabs), specify it with the `-Delimiter` parameter
- **Data Types:** PowerShell infers data types. Use the `-Header` parameter to provide your own if needed.

JSON (JavaScript Object Notation)

- **ConvertFrom-Json:** Your tool for turning JSON data back into PowerShell objects.

  ```
  $services = Get-Content -Path services.json |
  ConvertFrom-Json
  ```

- **Nested Data:** JSON's strength lies in representing complex structures that would be difficult in a flat CSV.

Handling API Results

Often, data from web services (REST APIs) is delivered as JSON:

```
$weatherData = Invoke-RestMethod -Uri
"https://api.openweathermap.org/data/2.5/weather?q=L
ondon&appid=YOUR_API_KEY"
$weatherData | ConvertFrom-Json
```

Tip: See upcoming chapters on 'Working with REST APIs' for a deeper dive into API interaction.

XML (Extensible Markup Language)

While less popular nowadays, XML still exists. PowerShell can handle it.

```
[xml]$xmlConfig = Get-Content .\configuration.xml
```

Important Note: Working with XML objects can be a bit more involved due to their hierarchical nature.

Additional Resources

- **ConvertFrom-Json Details:**
  https://docs.microsoft.com/en-us/powershell/module/microsoft.powershell.utility/convertfrom-json

Practice

1. **Process List from CSV**
   - Pretend a co-worker provided 'running_processes.csv'. Import it, then use `Where-Object` to find processes consuming more than 500MB of memory.
2. **Investigate a JSON API:**
   - Find a free public API (e.g., a weather API, or check https://any-api.com/).
   - Use PowerShell (`Invoke-RestMethod`) to call it and examine the JSON result.

Beyond the Basics

- **Text Files:** `Get-Content` for basic line-by-line reading.
- **Databases:** PowerShell can interact with many databases, but this requires specialized techniques and often additional modules.

- **Excel:** This also requires specialized techniques. You might explore the `ImportExcel` module (available on the PowerShell Gallery).

The Power of Import

Bringing in external data unlocks new automation scenarios:

- **Scripts Driven by Config Files:** Control script behavior through settings in a CSV, JSON, or XML file.
- **Reporting from External Data:** Combine live system data with an imported reference list for a comprehensive report.

Next: A Practice Challenge!

Let's solidify these skills with a hands-on challenge, where you'll combine formatting, saving, and importing techniques into a real-world automation solution.

Practice Challenge: Consolidating Your Knowledge – Part 1

Let's put your PowerShell data handling skills to the test! This chapter presents a scenario mirroring the types of tasks you might encounter in a real IT administration role.

The Challenge: Active Directory Account Cleanup

Your organization leverages Active Directory (AD). It's time to audit user accounts and disable those that haven't been used in over 90 days. Here's the breakdown:

Part 1: The Task

1. **Get Data (Hypothetical):** Since we can't interact with a live AD in this book, assume you have a CSV file named 'AD_accounts.csv' with the following columns:
   - Username
   - LastLogonDate (as a DateTime object)
   - Enabled (True/False)
2. **Identify Stale Accounts:** Filter for accounts where:
   - LastLogonDate is older than 90 days from today's date
   - Enabled is set to True
3. **Produce a Report:** Generate a new CSV named 'stale_accounts.csv' containing:
   - Username
   - DaysSinceLastLogon (Calculated – difference from today)

Part 2 (Next Chapter): We'll disable the accounts safely, but for now, focus on the data side.

Important Notes

- **Assume the CSV exists:** No need to create it—we're focusing on the PowerShell logic.
- **Date Calculations:** PowerShell has date-handling features (see Get-Date, the AddDays method).

- **Real-world Caveats:** Disabling AD accounts requires careful planning & potentially working with the AD cmdlets (an advanced topic).

Getting Started

1. **Import:** Use `Import-Csv` to load 'AD_accounts.csv' into a variable.
2. **Filtering:** Use `Where-Object` to find accounts matching the criteria. You might need multiple filter conditions:
   - LastLogonDate earlier than a calculated threshold
   - Enabled property is $true
3. **Calculated Properties:** Create a new object using `Select-Object` with calculations:
   - `DaysSinceLastLogon`: Logic to subtract LastLogonDate from today and get the timespan in days.
4. **Output:** Use `Export-Csv` to save your 'stale_accounts.csv' report.

Tips

- **Break It Down:** Solve one part at a time (import, filtering, calculations, export).
- **Test as You Go:** Create sample objects to experiment with filtering and date logic.
- **Pipeline Power:** Combine cmdlets step-by-step to build the solution.

Ready for Part 2?

In the next chapter, we'll take a sample solution and discuss not only how it works but also alternative approaches, ways to refine it, and the considerations of taking such a script into a production environment.

Practice Challenge: Solution Walkthrough – Part 2

Let's dive into a solution for our AD cleanup practice challenge! Remember, the goal is not a single perfect answer, but rather understanding techniques, decision points, and how to adapt the solution to your specific environment.

A Sample Solution (Let's Analyze):

```
# Sample 'AD_accounts.csv' is assumed.

$accounts = Import-Csv -Path 'AD_accounts.csv'
$staleThreshold = (Get-Date).AddDays(-90)

$staleAccounts = $accounts | Where-Object {
    $_.LastLogonDate -lt $staleThreshold -and $_.Enabled -eq
$true
} | Select-Object Username, @{Name='DaysSinceLastLogon';
Expression={($_.LastLogonDate - (Get-Date)).Days}}

$staleAccounts | Export-Csv -Path 'stale_accounts.csv'
-NoTypeInformation
```

Explanation

1. **Import and Threshold:** We import the CSV data and calculate the date 90 days in the past to mark our staleness boundary.
2. **Filtering with Where-Object:** We filter for accounts where both conditions hold:
   ○ `LastLogonDate` is older than our `$staleThreshold`
   ○ The `Enabled` property is `$true`
3. **Calculated Property:** Using `Select-Object`, we create a new object:
   ○ We keep the `Username`.
   ○ We calculate `DaysSinceLastLogon` by subtracting `LastLogonDate` from the current date and getting the total days.
4. **Export to CSV:** Our filtered and calculated data goes into 'stale_accounts.csv'.

Discussion Points

- **Clarity:** This solution is fairly concise. Can you add comments to make it even clearer for someone else to maintain?
- **Precision:** The date calculation is accurate but could be made a bit more readable, perhaps using the `New-Timespan` cmdlet.
- **Flexibility:** What if the "stale" period needs to change? Consider turning the "90" into a script parameter in a production scenario.

Beyond The Basics: Making it Production-Ready

- **Error Handling:** Imagine issues with the import file, or with setting account properties later on. A robust solution would use `try-catch` blocks.
- **Logging:** Instead of just a CSV, perhaps log which accounts were targeted *before* making changes.
- **Active Directory Cmdlets:** Disabling accounts likely involves the Active Directory PowerShell module. Research how to safely interact with AD objects.

Alternative Approaches

There are often several valid PowerShell solutions. Here's a stylistic variation:

```
$accounts | Where-Object { $_.Enabled -and
$_.LastLogonDate -lt (Get-Date).AddDays(-90) } |
    Select-Object -ExpandProperty Username |
    Add-Member -MemberType NoteProperty -Name
DaysSinceLastLogon -Value {
        ($_.LastLogonDate - (Get-Date)).Days
    } | Export-Csv ...
```

- **Add-Member:** This lets us dynamically add a calculated property to existing objects. Debate the pros and cons!

Real-World Considerations

- **Testing, testing!** Never run scripts that modify systems without testing on a non-production environment.

- **Permissions:** Ensure your script has the rights to both read and alter user accounts in Active Directory.

Key Takeaways

- **Solutions Evolve:** A first working solution is the start; you then enhance for readability, safety, and changing requirements.
- **There's More Than One Way:** PowerShell's flexibility means different styles can achieve the same goal.
- **Context is King:** The best solution in a production IT environment takes into account your specific AD setup, policies, and risk tolerance.

The Learning Continues

This practice challenge brings together essential skills. The more you use PowerShell for real-world tasks, the more fluent you'll become in combining its powerful toolset!

Section 4:
Functions and Scripting

Getting Started with the PowerShell ISE

Let's get acquainted with the PowerShell Integrated Scripting Environment (ISE)! It's a powerful tool that can significantly enhance your scripting and development experience. While the basic PowerShell console is great for commands and quick tasks, the ISE brings your scripting to the next level. Let's explore its features and how to make the most of them.

What is the PowerShell ISE?

- **More than an Editor:** It goes beyond basic code editing, providing:
    - A multi-tabbed interface for working on several scripts at once.
    - Integrated console for testing and execution.
    - Rich debugging features.
    - Syntax highlighting and help integration.

Launching the ISE

There are a few ways to find it:

- **Start Menu:** Search for "PowerShell ISE".
- **Run Dialog:** Press Windows Key + R, and type "powershell_ise.exe".
- **Within the Console:** You can type `ise` from a regular PowerShell console.

The ISE Layout

1. **Script Pane:** The top portion is your primary code editor.

2. **Console Pane:** The bottom pane is a fully functional PowerShell console, where your scripts run and output is displayed.
3. **Command Add-on (Optional):** A pane to the right that aids discovery of available cmdlets. We'll focus less on this as understanding core PowerShell is most important.

Basic Authoring

- **New Scripts:** Click "New" (or File -> New), or Ctrl + N.
- **Save Scripts:** Click "Save" (or File -> Save), or Ctrl + S. Always save as `.ps1` files!
- **Running Code:**
  - Press F5 to run the entire script in your editor.
  - Select a portion of code and press F8 to run only the selected part.

Syntax Highlighting

- **Colors Mean Something:** The ISE colorizes keywords, variables, strings, and more, improving code readability.
- **Customization:** You can adjust these colors under Tools -> Options if you wish.

Integrated Help

- **Get-Help in the ISE:** Use the `Get-Help` cmdlet directly in the console pane. Results display conveniently alongside your code.
- **ISE Command Browser:** If the Command Add-on pane is visible, it offers an alternative way to explore cmdlet help.

Debugging Features

The ISE helps you find and fix issues in your scripts:

- **Breakpoints:** Click the margin next to a line to set a breakpoint. Your script will pause there when run (F5).
- **Stepping Through Code:** While paused at a breakpoint, use:
  - F10 to step over a line (execute without going inside functions).
  - F11 to step into a function call.

○ Shift + F11 to step out of the current function.

- **Examining Variables:** Hover over variables to see their values when the script is paused, or use the console pane to inspect them.

Additional Resources

- **ISE Overview (Microsoft Docs):** https://docs.microsoft.com/en-us/powershell/scripting/windows-powershell/ise/introducing-the-windows-powershell-ise

Practice Makes Perfect

1. **Experiment:** Open the ISE and try the following:
   - Type a simple script (e.g., `Write-Output "Hello, ISE!"`) and run it.
   - Set a breakpoint and practice stepping through the code line by line.
2. **Explore the Interface:** Click around the menus and see what options are available. Don't be afraid to experiment!

Key Points

- **ISE vs. Code:** Later, we'll cover Visual Studio Code, an even more advanced editor. For beginners, the ISE offers a smooth learning curve.
- **Customization:** The ISE is customizable (layout, colors, etc.).
- **Workflow:** The ISE encourages you to write a bit of code, test it immediately, and iterate – a powerful development cycle.

Next: Building Your First Function!

Now that you're comfortable with the ISE, we're ready to start organizing your PowerShell code into reusable functions!

Building Your First Function – Part 1

Let's embark on the exciting world of PowerShell functions. These are the building blocks that allow you to create reusable, modular, and well-organized scripts, taking your PowerShell skills to the next level.

Why Functions Matter

1. **Reusability:** Write a piece of code once, use it many times. This saves time and effort in the long run.
2. **Organization:** Functions break down complex scripts into smaller, manageable chunks, making code easier to read and maintain.
3. **Abstraction:** Functions let you hide implementation details and provide a simple interface to perform a task. This makes your scripts easier for others (or your future self) to use.

Basic Function Structure

Here's the simplest form of a PowerShell function:

```
function Get-Greeting {
    "Hello, from my first function!"
}
```

Let's break it down:

- **function:** The keyword that tells PowerShell you're defining a function.
- **Get-Greeting:** The name of your function. Naming often follows a Verb-Noun pattern.
- **{ }** Curly braces enclose the code that your function will execute.

Using Your Function

In the ISE, type `Get-Greeting` and press Enter to call it. You should see the output!

Real-World Example: Getting Process Info

```
function Get-ProcessInfo {
    Param(
```

```
        [string]$Name
    )

    Get-Process -Name $Name | Select-Object Name,
Id, WorkingSet
}
```

Explanation

- **Param():** This block (optional, but highly recommended) is where you'll define input parameters later on. For now, we'll take a single process name.
- **Get-Process -Name $Name:** We filter for processes matching the given name.
- **Select-Object:** We choose specific properties to neatly display.

Using the Enhanced Function

1. **Type:** `Get-ProcessInfo notepad` (if Notepad is running).
2. **Output:** You'll get a nicely formatted table with the process's name, ID, and memory usage.

Key Points

- **Function Naming:** Verb-Noun names help with code readability (`Get-ProcessInfo` is clearer than something like `procdata`)
- **Scope:** Functions, by default, exist only in your current session. Saving them in scripts makes them persistent. (Covered later)

Additional Resources

- **All About Functions:**
  https://docs.microsoft.com/en-us/powershell/module/microsoft.powershell.core/about/about_functions

Practice Time!

1. **Write a Simple Function:** Create a function named `Get-TodaysDate` that outputs the current date in a short format (e.g., MM/DD/YYYY).

2. **Function for File Size:** Write a function called `Get-FileSize` that takes a file path as input and then displays the file size in KB.
   - Hint: You might need properties from the `Get-Item` cmdlet.

Coming Up: Parameters

So far, our functions have been a bit rigid. In the next chapter, we'll introduce parameters that make our functions flexible and adaptable to different scenarios.

Building Your First Function – Part 2

Let's continue our journey into functions and introduce parameters – the key to making your functions dynamic and truly reusable!

Parameters: Inputs for Flexibility

Think of parameters as variables that live within your function and are supplied when you call it. Let's revamp our `Get-ProcessInfo` example:

```
function Get-ProcessInfo {
    Param(
        [string]$Name
    )

    Get-Process -Name $Name | Select-Object Name,
Id, WorkingSet
}
```

- **Inside the Param() Block:** We declare a single parameter named $Name and specify its data type as a string.

Using the Parameterized Function

Now, instead of being hardcoded, our function expects input:

1. **Call It:** `Get-ProcessInfo -Name chrome`
2. **Flexibility:** You can easily substitute "chrome" for any other process name.

Key Points About Parameters

- **Order vs. Naming:** You can either supply parameters in the correct order (`Get-ProcessInfo notepad`), or specify the parameter name directly (`Get-ProcessInfo -Name notepad`).
- **Types Matter:** PowerShell will try to convert input to the declared parameter type. Be careful if you expect numbers!

More Parameter Power

Let's make `Get-ProcessInfo` even better:

```
function Get-ProcessInfo {
    Param(
        [string]$Name,
        [switch]$IncludeDescription
    )

    $filter = @{Name = $Name}

    Get-Process @filter |
        Select-Object Name, Id, WorkingSet,
                      @{Name='Description';
Expression={$_.Description}} -First 1

    if ($IncludeDescription) {
        Write-Output "`nDescription Available"
    }
}
```

Changes

1. **New Parameter:** `$IncludeDescription` is a switch parameter. If present, it triggers additional behavior in the function.
2. **Conditional Output:** We include the description and an extra message only if `$IncludeDescription` is used.
3. **Dynamic Filter:** For more complex scenarios, this shows how parameters can be used to build properties for other cmdlets.

How to Use the Enhanced Version

- **Basics:** `Get-ProcessInfo -Name svchost`
- **Details:** `Get-ProcessInfo -Name svchost -IncludeDescription`

Additional Resources

- **Even More on Parameters:**
  https://docs.microsoft.com/en-us/powershell/module/microsoft.powershell.core/about/about_functions_advanced_parameters

Practice

1. **Modify Get-FileSize:** Update the `Get-FileSize` function you wrote previously to take a mandatory file path parameter as input.
2. **Parameterized Report:**
   - Write a function `Get-LargeFiles` that takes a folder path and file size threshold (in KB) as parameters.
   - Report on files in that folder exceeding the size threshold.

Beyond Simple Parameters

- **Default Values:** Make parameters optional.
- **Parameter Validation:** Enforce specific input conditions for your parameters.
- **Pipeline Input:** We'll cover these in future chapters, making functions integrate seamlessly with PowerShell workflows.

Advanced Functions: Parameters and External Cmdlets – Part 1

Let's dive deeper into the realm of PowerShell functions! This chapter explores how they become even more powerful through advanced parameter techniques and by seamlessly interacting with the vast world of PowerShell cmdlets.

Parameters for Control

Let's enhance our file reporting function from previous chapters:

```
function Get-LargeFiles {
    Param(
        [string]$FolderPath,
        [int]$SizeThresholdKB = 1024, # 1 MB Default
        [switch]$Recurse
    )

    $params = @{
        Path = $FolderPath
        File = $true
    }

    if ($Recurse) { $params.Add('Recurse', $true) }

    Get-ChildItem @params |
        Where-Object { $_.Length -gt
($SizeThresholdKB * 1KB) } |
        Select-Object FullName, Length
}
```

New Features

1. **Default Value:** Our $SizeThresholdKB now has a default of 1MB. This means the function works even if the parameter isn't provided.
2. **Recurse Switch:** Changes the search to include subfolders if desired.
3. **Splatting for Dynamic Parameters:**

- ○ We build a `$params` hashtable to hold arguments for `Get-ChildItem`.
- ○ 'Splatting' (using `@params`) is a convenient way to pass these to cmdlets.

Using the Enhanced Version

- **Simple Search:** `Get-LargeFiles -FolderPath C:\Reports` (uses the 1 MB default threshold)
- **Bigger Files:** `Get-LargeFiles -FolderPath C:\Downloads -SizeThresholdKB 5120` (looks for files larger than 5GB)
- **Recursive and Smaller Limit:** `Get-LargeFiles -FolderPath C:\Temp -SizeThresholdKB 100 -Recurse`

Functions Calling Functions (and Cmdlets!)

The beauty of PowerShell is that functions and cmdlets are all part of the same ecosystem. Let's create a function to stop services:

```
function Stop-ServiceSafely {
    Param(
        [string]$ServiceName
    )

    if (Get-Service -Name $ServiceName |
Where-Object {$_.Status -eq 'Running'}) {
        Stop-Service -Name $ServiceName -Force
        Write-Output "Service $ServiceName stopped."
    } else {
        Write-Output "Service $ServiceName is not
currently running."
    }
}
```

Notice:

- **Function Inside a Function:** We're using `Get-Service` to help with the logic of when to stop the service.

- **Force:** For IT scenarios, sometimes it's necessary to forcefully stop a service. Use this parameter with caution!

Key Points

- **Modular Design:** Smaller functions focused on specific tasks make complex scripts easier to build and maintain.
- **Functions as Building Blocks:** Break down automation problems into smaller steps, each solvable by a function or cmdlet.

Pipeline Power

Functions can integrate directly with the PowerShell pipeline, making data flow seamlessly. Suppose we want to restart the top 5 memory-consuming processes:

```
Get-Process | Sort-Object WorkingSet -Descending |
    Select-Object -First 5 |
    Restart-Service # Assuming a hypothetical
'Restart-Service'
```

Building a Pipeline-Ready Function

The key is the `process` pipeline parameter:

```
function Resize-Image {
    [CmdletBinding()]
    Param(
        [Parameter(ValueFromPipeline)]
        [System.IO.FileInfo]$File
    )

    process {
        # Image modification logic using $File...
    }
}
```

- **[CmdletBinding()]:** This attribute enables advanced parameter features.

- **[Parameter(ValueFromPipeline)]:** Allows our function to accept objects directly from the pipeline.
- **process Block:** This is where you process each incoming $File object.

Practice

1. **Modify Get-LargeFiles:** Add a sorting parameter to control the order of the reported files (e.g., by name, size, ascending/descending).
2. **Pipeline-Friendly Function:**
   - Write a function called Add-DateStamp that takes a file as input and appends the current date and time to the filename.
   - Test: Get-ChildItem *.txt | Add-DateStamp

Next: Even More Parameter Techniques!

PowerShell offers ways to validate parameter input, accept pipeline input by property name, and much more. These techniques are essential for robust scripts used in production environments.

Advanced Functions: Parameters and External Cmdlets – Part 2

In this chapter, we'll cover techniques to make your functions more robust, adaptable, and production-ready.

Parameter Validation

Ensure your functions receive the correct input to avoid unexpected errors:

```
function Start-ScheduledTaskSafely {
    Param(
        [Parameter(Mandatory)]
        [ValidateScript({ Test-Path $_ -PathType
Leaf })] # Must be an existing file
        [string]$TaskScriptPath
    )

    # ... rest of the function ...
}
```

- **Mandatory:** Parameters that *must* be provided are marked as mandatory.
- **ValidateScript:** This lets you attach a script block to test input. Here, we ensure $TaskScriptPath points to a real file.

More Validation Techniques

- **ValidateSet:** Restrict input to a fixed set of allowed values.
- **ValidateRange:** Enforce that a number falls within a specific range.
- **ValidatePattern:** Use regular expressions for complex input rules.

Pipeline Input: The Other Way

Sometimes you want functions to accept objects from the pipeline based on a specific property:

```
function Update-ServiceDescription {
    [CmdletBinding()]
    Param(
        [Parameter(Mandatory,
ValueFromPipelineByProperty)]
        [string]$Name,
        [string]$Description
    )

    process {
        Set-Service -Name $Name -Description
$Description
    }
}
```

- **ValueFromPipelineByProperty:** Indicates the function takes input based on the 'Name' property of incoming objects.

Example Usage

```
Get-Service Spooler, BITS |
Update-ServiceDescription -Description "New
Description Here"
```

Output Considerations

Think carefully about what your functions should output:

- **Return Values for Calculations:** If your function does a calculation, return the result (Get-TotalFileSize -Folder 'C:\Reports').
- **Objects for Pipelines:** Functions intended for pipeline workflows should output modified objects for the next stage to consume.
- **Sometimes, Nothing:** Actions like stopping a service might simply output status messages using Write-Output rather than returning an object.

Advanced Parameter Scenarios

We'll just mention these briefly (a full exploration is quite in-depth):

- **Parameter Sets:** Create groups of parameters that are mutually exclusive, used for functions that have multiple modes of operation.
- **Dynamic Parameters:** Parameters that are revealed based on the values of other parameters in your function.

Additional Resources

- **'about_Functions_Advanced_Parameters':** https://docs.microsoft.com/en-us/powershell/module/microsoft.powershell.core/about/about_functions_advanced_parameters

Practice

1. **Robust Parameter:** Enhance your `Get-LargeFiles` function to include validation, ensuring the `SizeThresholdKB` is a positive number.
2. **Pipeline by Property:**
   - Write a function `Set-FileOwner` that takes pipeline input and updates a file's owner.
   - It should accept input by property name 'FullName'.

Key Takeaways

- **Input Control:** Validation helps you write functions that behave predictably, crucial when scripts are used by others or in automated tasks.
- **Pipeline Power & Design:** Consider how a function fits within a broader PowerShell workflow. Does it process input objects? Calculate values? The design follows from this understanding.

Up Next: Scripting!

With powerful functions at our disposal, we're ready to take the next step and learn how to assemble them into full-fledged PowerShell scripts – the heart of real-world automation tasks.

Writing Your First PowerShell Script

Let's embark on the transition from individual functions to structured PowerShell scripts, where automation truly takes shape.

From Functions to Scripts

- **Functions: The Building Blocks:** Functions encapsulate specific tasks, promoting code reusability and maintainability.
- **Scripts: The Orchestrators:** Scripts bring together functions, cmdlets, logic, and control flow to achieve larger automation goals.

A Simple Starter Script

```
# A basic backup status reporting script

function Get-TodaysDate {
    (Get-Date).ToString('yyyy-MM-dd')
}


$backupFolder = "D:\Backups"
$todaysDate = Get-TodaysDate()
$logFile = Join-Path $backupFolder
"BackupLog_$todaysDate.txt"

if (Test-Path -Path $logFile) {
    Write-Output "Backup log found for today."
} else {
    Write-Warning "No backup log for today! Check
the backup process."
}
```

Breakdown

1. **Function:** We're reusing our handy date function.
2. **Variables:** Store key paths for clarity.
3. **Logic (if/else):** The core decision making of the script.
4. **Join-Path:** Safely constructs a file path.
5. **Output:** User-friendly status messages.

Executing Your Script

1. **Save as .ps1:** Save the code with a .ps1 file extension (e.g., BackupStatusCheck.ps1).
2. **From the ISE:** Press F5 to run the entire script within the ISE.
3. **From PowerShell Console:**
   - Navigate to the script's location.
   - Type .\BackupStatusCheck.ps1 (note the '.') and press Enter.

Key Scripting Concepts

- **Comments (Lines starting with #):** Explain your code's logic for future reference (both to yourself and others).
- **Order Matters:** Generally, scripts are executed from top to bottom, but you'll soon learn about control flow structures (loops, branches).

Expanding Your Script

Let's enhance our script:

```
# ... (Previous code remains the same)


# Add error checking for the backup folder itself
if (-not (Test-Path $backupFolder)) {
    Write-Error "Backup folder not found. Please
investigate!" -ErrorAction Stop
}


# Add a success message when the log file exists
if (Test-Path -Path $logFile) {
    Write-Output "Backup log found for today.
Success!"
} else {
    # ... (Previous 'no backup log' logic)
}
```

New Things

- **Error Handling:** We use `Write-Error` to signal a critical issue and `-ErrorAction Stop` to halt the script immediately.
- **Success Message:** Enhancements don't always have to be about failures!

Additional Resources

- **About Scripting:**
  https://docs.microsoft.com/en-us/powershell/scripting/overview

Practice

1. **File Cleanup Script:** Write a script that:
   - Asks the user for a folder path.
   - Finds files in that folder older than 30 days.
   - Reports on these files, giving the option to delete them.
2. **Refactoring Your Functions:** If you have functions written in previous exercises, turn them into a simple script with a menu. For instance:
   - Option 1: Get large files in a folder.
   - Option 2: Stop a service.

Section 5:
Project – Automating File Organization with PowerShell

Project Overview

Let's dive into the foundation of our file organization project. This chapter will outline the problem we're solving, the goals we aim to achieve, and the high-level design of our PowerShell solution.

The Challenge: File and Folder Chaos

In many IT environments, file management can become a source of headaches. Consider these scenarios:

- **Important Documents Scattered:** Project files, reports, or critical data end up dispersed across network shares, personal drives, and forgotten folders.
- **Aging Files Hogging Space:** Old archives, temporary files, and redundant backups consume valuable storage.
- **Lack of Structure:** Inconsistent naming conventions and haphazard folder hierarchies make finding what you need a frustrating treasure hunt.

Project Goal: Bringing Order with PowerShell

Our mission is to build a PowerShell script that addresses these common file organization pain points. Core objectives include:

1. **Targeted Cleanup:** Identifying and removing files based on criteria like:
   - Age (older than X days)
   - File types (e.g., .tmp, .log)
   - Size thresholds

2. **Intelligent Archiving:** Moving files matching specific patterns to designated archive locations based on rules we define.
3. **Comprehensive Reporting:** Generating reports detailing:
   - The actions taken (files deleted, moved)
   - Total space reclaimed
   - Potential areas for further optimization

Script Design: A Modular Approach

We'll achieve this using the power of functions and PowerShell's flexibility:

- **Folder Verification Function:** Ensures a provided folder path exists and is accessible.
- **File Statistics Function:** Calculates statistics like the number of files, total size, and identifies the largest files within a folder.
- **Core Processing Logic:** This is where we'll implement the rules for deletion, archival, and govern how the script interacts with the file system.

Benefits of this Project

- **Save Time:** Automate tasks that would be tedious and error-prone if done manually.
- **Free Up Storage:** Recover valuable disk space without sacrificing important data.
- **Improve Findability:** Bring a sense of order, simplifying how users locate the files they need.
- **PowerShell Mastery:** Sharpen your scripting skills by tackling a real-world IT administration problem.

Considerations

- **Scope:** Start with a focused scope. Perhaps we'll initially handle file deletion and basic reporting, later expanding into archiving.
- **Testing: Always** test on non-critical folders before deploying a script like this into a production environment.
- **User Input (Later):** We could enhance the script to take parameters, customizing its behavior for different scenarios.

Additional Resources

- **Filesystem Cmdlets:** These will be our workhorses: https://docs.microsoft.com/en-us/powershell/module/microsoft.powershell.management/?view=powershell-7.2

Practice (Optional)

- **Start Thinking Functionally:** Sketch out some rough function names and the kinds of information they might take as input or produce as output. Example: `Remove-OldFiles`

Ready to Dive In

In the next chapter, we'll begin constructing the first key component, our folder verification function. A robust foundation will ensure our script works safely and reliably.

Defining the Scope

Let's solidify the boundaries and focus of our file organization project. A well-defined scope is crucial for any scripting endeavor, preventing us from getting lost in endless features and ensuring our solution delivers tangible value.

Why Scope Matters

- **Clarity:** A clear scope keeps you on track, especially as your project and the script's capabilities grow.
- **Time Management:** Avoid 'scope creep', where projects expand uncontrollably, leading to delays and frustration.
- **Prioritization:** Lets you tackle the most impactful features first.

Phase 1: Core Functionality

Our initial scope will center around these fundamental tasks:

1. **Folder Validation:**
   - Users provide a folder path.
   - Verify the folder exists.
   - Ensure the script has permissions to access it.
2. **Deletion Based on Age:**
   - Find files older than a configurable number of days.
   - Securely delete these files.
3. **Basic Reporting:**
   - Log deleted filenames.
   - Display the total amount of disk space freed up.

Decisions and Trade-offs

- **File Types:** For phase 1, we'll focus on *age* as the primary deletion criterion. Later, we could add filtering by file extensions.
- **Archiving vs. Deletion:** Initially, we're deleting. Archiving (moving files) is more complex (where to move them?) and is a great phase 2 addition.
- **UI (User Interface):** To start, we might take folder paths as simple script input. A fancy graphical interface is a possibility much later!

Flexibility for Growth: Parameters

Even in this initial scope, let's plan for expandability:

- **-FolderPath:** A parameter to specify the target folder.
- **-DaysOld:** A parameter controlling the age threshold for deletion.

Scope Considerations

1. **Target Environment:**
   - Network shares vs. local drives?
   - Windows versions? (Affects some file system interactions)
2. **Specific Pain Points:** Are temporary files a major culprit? Are certain file types cluttering known folders? This can guide future script enhancements.

What We're NOT Doing (Yet)

- **Undelete:** No 'recycle bin' functionality at this stage.
- **Complex File Type Scanning:** Identifying files based on their contents (e.g., finding duplicate MP3s) is outside our current scope.
- **Scheduled Execution:** We'll focus on running the script manually for now. Automation as a scheduled task is a logical next step.

Practice

- **Envision Phase 2:** Assuming phase 1 is a success, jot down 2-3 features you'd most want to add in the next phase of development.

The Value of Iteration

Software development (and scripting!) is often an iterative process. A well-defined initial scope lets us deliver value quickly, and then gather feedback to intelligently guide where to expand the script's capabilities next.

Setting Up Parameters

Let's talk about parameters, the key to making our file organization script flexible and adaptable to different scenarios.

Why Parameters Are Your Friend

1. **Avoid Hardcoding:** Instead of embedding values like folder paths directly in the script, parameters let us provide them at runtime.
2. **Reusability:** A well-parameterized script can clean up different folders, target different age limits, and much more, all without changing the code itself.
3. **Future You:** Even if you're the only one using the script now, parameters make it much easier to understand and reuse it months later.

Our Parameters

Let's revisit our scope and define the initial parameters:

- **-FolderPath <string> (Mandatory):** The path to the folder the script should operate on. Mandatory means the script won't run without it.
- **-DaysOld <int> (Optional):** The age threshold in days. Files older than this will be considered for deletion. We'll provide a sensible default value.

Basic Parameter Declaration

Start a new script file (e.g., FileCleanup.ps1). Inside it, add a param() block at the very top:

```
param(
    [Parameter(Mandatory)]
    [string]$FolderPath,

    [int]$DaysOld = 30 # Default of 30 days
)
```

Understanding the Syntax

- **[Parameter(Mandatory)]:** Indicates when a parameter *must* be provided.
- **[string] / [int]:** These specify the expected data types for our parameters. PowerShell will try to convert the input to the correct type.
- **= 30:** Assigns a default value to $DaysOld.

Test It Out (ISE)

1. **Type in the param block:** Just the declaration as shown above.
2. **Run (F5):** The ISE will prompt you for the values of FolderPath and DaysOld since the latter has a default, it'll be pre-filled.

Using Parameters in Your Script

Inside your script, you now have variables $FolderPath and $DaysOld that you can use directly. We'll replace any hardcoded paths or values with these.

Example: A Tiny Script

```
param(
    [Parameter(Mandatory)]
    [string]$FolderPath
)

Write-Output "Target Folder: $FolderPath"
```

Considerations

- **Naming:** Descriptive names make your script self-documenting (-CleanupThresholdDays is clearer than just -Days).
- **Validation:** In later chapters, we'll learn how to ensure parameters meet specific criteria (ValidateRange for example).

Additional Resources

- **All About Parameters:**
  https://docs.microsoft.com/en-us/powershell/module/microsoft.powershell.core/about/about_functions_advanced_parameters

Practice

1. **Add a Parameter:** Think of another parameter that would be useful for our file cleanup script. Options include:
   - File size limit (delete files larger than X).
   - File extension filter (e.g., `-FileTypes '*.tmp'`, `'*.log'`).
2. **Experiment:** Try running your script in the ISE *without* providing all the mandatory parameters. Observe the error messages.

The Power of Flexibility

Parameters seem simple, but they're foundational. As our script gains features, the ability to control its behavior through parameters will become essential for its usefulness in real-world tasks.

Coming Up Next

We now have a way to get input into our script. The next step is our first essential function: folder verification!

Folder Verification Function – Part 1

Let's get started on building the cornerstone of our file organization script – a function to ensure we're always working with a valid, accessible folder. This chapter will focus on the core folder checks.

The Importance of a Good Foundation

Imagine your script deleting files in the wrong location – yikes! Our folder verification function helps prevent these disasters:

- **Existence:** Does the provided folder path actually point to a real folder?
- **Permissions:** Can our script read the folder's contents and (if it's going to delete things) make changes within it?
- **Readiness:** Is the folder on a local drive, a network share, etc.? This might influence how we interact with it later.

Our Function: Start Simple

```
function Verify-FolderPath {
    param(
        [Parameter(Mandatory)]
        [string]$FolderPath
    )


    # Basic Existence Check
    if (Test-Path -Path $FolderPath) {
        Write-Output "Folder exists: $FolderPath"
    } else {
        Write-Error "Folder not found: $FolderPath"
-ErrorAction Stop
    }
}
```

Let's break it down:

1. **Verify-FolderPath:** A descriptive name (Verb-Noun).
2. **The param() Block:** Our now familiar way to take input.

3. **Test-Path:** This handy cmdlet checks if a path exists.
4. **if/else:** Simple branching logic for now.
5. **Write-Output:** For success messages.
6. **Write-Error:** For critical errors. `-ErrorAction Stop` halts the entire script if verification fails.

Using the Function (Temporarily)

Add this function to your `FileCleanup.ps1` script and put the following line *somewhere after it*:

```
Verify-FolderPath -FolderPath "C:\SomeFolder"
```

Testing in the ISE

1. **Run (F5):** If the folder exists, you'll get the output message.
2. **Change the FolderPath to something nonexistent:** You'll get the error and the script will stop.

Beyond Basic Existence

Let's enhance our function:

```
# ... (Existing code from above) ...

    # Check if it's a file system folder
    if (Test-Path -Path $FolderPath -PathType
Container) {
        # More checks to come...
    } else {
        Write-Error "$FolderPath is not a valid file
system folder." -ErrorAction Stop
    }
}
```

- **-PathType Container:** This ensures we're working with a true folder, not accidentally a file.

Additional Resources

- **About Test-Path:**
  https://docs.microsoft.com/en-us/powershell/module/microsoft.powershell.management/test-path
- **Error Handling (We'll revisit this in depth later):**
  https://docs.microsoft.com/en-us/powershell/module/microsoft.powershell.core/about/about_try_catch_finally

Practice

- **Imagine a Mishap:** Write a 1-2 sentence scenario of how your script could cause unintended damage *without* a good folder verification function.

Coming Up: Permissions and More

So far, we're making sure the folder exists. Next, we'll tackle permission checks to be certain our script is actually *allowed* to do its work within that folder.

Folder Verification Function – Part 2

Let's complete our robust `Verify-FolderPath` function, focusing on the crucial aspect of permissions and ensuring the script has the necessary rights to do its job.

Understanding Permissions

- **FileSystem Access:** In Windows, permissions (part of the NTFS security model) control which users and groups can:
    - Read a folder's contents.
    - Create new files or subfolders within it.
    - Delete things inside the folder.
- **Script's Identity:** PowerShell scripts generally run under the permissions of the user who launched them. This matters!

Checking Permissions (a Bit Tricky)

There's no single cmdlet like `Test-FolderPermissions`. We'll use a .NET method to help:

```
function Verify-FolderPath {
    # ... (Our existing code) ...

    # Permissions (rough first attempt)
    $folder = Get-Item -Path $FolderPath
    $acl = $folder.GetAccessControl()

    try {
        # Try to modify the folder's security (this
can throw exceptions)
        $acl.SetAccessRuleProtection($true, $false)
        $folder.SetAccessControl($acl)
        Write-Output "Script appears to have the
necessary permissions."
    } catch {
        Write-Error "Error checking folder
permissions: $FolderPath. Ensure your account has
modify rights." -ErrorAction Stop
```

```
        }
}
```

Explanation

1. **`Get-Item` + `GetAccessControl()`:** We fetch the folder's Access Control List (ACL), which holds permission rules.
2. **The `try/catch` Block:** Crucial for this kind of operation:
   - **Inside the `try`:** We attempt a minor modification to the folder's security settings. If our script has write permissions, this will succeed silently.
   - **If it fails...:** The `catch` block is triggered, indicating our script likely *doesn't* have the permissions it needs.

Important Considerations

- **User Context:** If the script will be run by regular users (not admins), they'll need appropriate permissions on the folders it will be managing.
- **Auditing:** For production use, consider logging the detailed contents of the `$acl` variable. This can aid in troubleshooting permissions.

Beyond the Basics

A production-ready function might also check:

- **Network Shares:** Folders on remote systems might have different permission requirements.
- **Specific Rights:** Do we need only 'read', or also the ability to delete and create files? We could refine the check.

Function in Action (Updated)

Within your `FileCleanup.ps1`:

```
# Our fully enhanced Verify-FolderPath function

Verify-FolderPath -FolderPath "C:\Temp"    # Should
succeed (normal case)
```

```
Verify-FolderPath -FolderPath "C:\Windows"  # Likely
to fail
```

Additional Resources

- **.NET File/Folder Permissions:**
  https://docs.microsoft.com/en-us/dotnet/api/system.io.file
- **'try/catch':**
  https://docs.microsoft.com/en-us/powershell/module/microsoft.powershell.core/about/about_try_catch_finally

Practice

- **Test Thoroughly:** Experiment with your function on folders where you know regular users *do* and *don't* have full control. Observe the script's behavior.

Building on a Solid Base

Our `Verify-FolderPath` function is now laying the groundwork for a script we can trust. If folder validation fails, we've saved ourselves from potential errors or even accidental data loss further down the line.

Next Up: File Statistics

With verification in place, we're ready to build a function that gathers statistics about the contents of our target folder – file sizes, counts, and more!

Folder Statistics Function – Part 1

Let's dive into building a function to analyze folder contents. This information will be key for our file cleanup decisions!

The Purpose of File Statistics

Our function will be tasked with answering questions like:

- **Overall Size:** How much space does the folder (and its subfolders) consume?
- **File Counts:** How many files are within the folder structure?
- **Largest Files:** What are the top space-hogging files? This is useful for targeting cleanup.

Designing the Function

```
function Get-FolderStatistics {
    param(
        [Parameter(Mandatory)]
        [string]$FolderPath
    )

    $stats = [PSCustomObject]@{
        FolderPath        = $FolderPath
        TotalFileCount    = 0
        TotalSizeInBytes  = 0
        LargestFiles      = @()
    }

    # To be filled in...

    return $stats
}
```

Explanation

1. **Get-FolderStatistics:** A descriptive name.

2. **$stats:** We'll create a custom object to hold our results. This makes outputting the statistics neat and easy.
3. **[PSCustomObject]:** PowerShell's way of creating objects with specific properties.
4. **Placeholders:** We initialize properties; the real calculation will happen soon!

The Core Calculation

Let's focus on the core file enumeration logic:

```
# ... Inside the function ...

Get-ChildItem -Path $FolderPath -Recurse -File |
ForEach-Object {
    $stats.TotalFileCount++
    $stats.TotalSizeInBytes += $_.Length

    # Logic to track largest files will come
later...
}
```

- **Get-ChildItem ... -File:** Efficiently gets all files within the folder and its subfolders.
- **ForEach-Object:** Lets us process each file individually.
- **Updating the $stats object:** We increment the file count and add to the total size with each file encountered.

Using the Function (Simple Example)

```
# Assuming our Verify-FolderPath function exists
from previous chapters...
Verify-FolderPath -FolderPath 'C:\Windows\Temp'

$folderStats = Get-FolderStatistics -FolderPath
'C:\Windows\Temp'
$folderStats  # Output the gathered statistics
```

Output Right Now

You'd see the folder path, a file count, and a total size. The
`LargestFiles` property would still be empty.

Additional Resources

- **Get-ChildItem:**
  https://docs.microsoft.com/en-us/powershell/module/microsoft.pow
  ershell.management/get-childitem

Practice

- **Test it Out:** Run the function on a smaller folder with a known
  number of files to verify the count and size seem correct.

Coming Up: Largest Files

Calculating basic stats is a good start, but the `LargestFiles` is where
things get interesting for cleanup tasks. In the next part, we'll tackle
finding those space-hungry culprits!

Folder Statistics Function – Part 2

Let's complete our `Get-FolderStatistics` function by adding the ability to identify the largest files, giving us actionable targets for our file cleanup script.

Finding the Top Offenders

Inside our `Get-FolderStatistics` function, within the `Get-ChildItem` loop, add the following:

```
# ... Inside the ForEach-Object loop ...

    if ($stats.LargestFiles.Count -lt 10) {
        $stats.LargestFiles += $_
    } else {
        # Find the smallest file among the current
top 10
        $smallest = $stats.LargestFiles |
Sort-Object Length | Select-Object -First 1

        # If the current file is bigger, replace
        if ($_.Length -gt $smallest.Length) {
            $stats.LargestFiles.Remove($smallest)
            $stats.LargestFiles += $_
        }
    }
}
```

Let's break this down

1. **Limiting to Top 10:** We keep track of the 10 largest files encountered so far. You could make this configurable if you like!
2. **Array Logic:** If we haven't yet filled our `LargestFiles` array, we simply add the current file.
3. **Finding the Smallest:** Once we're tracking 10 files, we use `Sort-Object` to find the smallest among them.
4. **Replacement:** If the file we're processing is *bigger* than the smallest currently tracked file, we swap them out.

Efficiency Note

This continuously maintains a top-10 list. A more memory-efficient way would be to process *all* files, then sort once at the end, but for typical file cleanup scenarios, this approach is suitable.

Outputting the Largest

After the loop, let's enhance the output of our function:

```
# ... After the Get-ChildItem loop ...

$stats.LargestFiles | Sort-Object Length -Descending
| Select-Object Name, Length
```

Using the Enhanced Function

Call the function like before:

```
$folderStats = Get-FolderStatistics -FolderPath
'C:\SomeFolder'
$folderStats
```

You'll now see the folder path, size, counts, *and* a table of the largest files!

Considerations

- **Output Formatting:** Later, we might send this data to a CSV file or create an HTML report for easy viewing.
- **Speed:** On folders with *huge* numbers of files, getting statistics might get a little slow. There are some optimizations if this becomes a bottleneck.

Additional Resources

- **Arrays:**
  https://docs.microsoft.com/en-us/powershell/scripting/learn/deep-dives/everything-about-arrays
- **Sorting Objects:**
  https://docs.microsoft.com/en-us/powershell/module/microsoft.powershell.utility/sort-object

116

Practice

- **Modify the Limit:** Change the logic to track the top 5 or top 20 largest files.

Power in Your Hands

Our `Get-FolderStatistics` function is now a powerful analytical tool. It provides the data we'll need to make informed decisions about what files to target for deletion in our script's core logic.

Next Up: It's Cleanup Time!

With verification and statistics in place, we're ready to tackle the heart of our script: the logic governing file deletion based on criteria like age and size.

Core Processing Logic – Part 1

Let's get to the heart of our file cleanup script! In this chapter, we'll tackle the central logic that determines which files get deleted based on our chosen criteria.

Design: A New Function

We'll encapsulate the processing logic into a function. Let's start with a basic outline:

```
function Process-FolderForCleanup {
    param(
        [Parameter(Mandatory)]
        [string]$FolderPath,
        [Parameter(Mandatory)]
        [int]$DaysOld
    )


    # Logic to find and process files for deletion
will go here...
}
```

Inside the Function (Iteration 1)

Let's begin with the age-based deletion logic:

```
# ... Inside the function ...

Get-ChildItem -Path $FolderPath -Recurse -File |
Where-Object {
        $_.LastWriteTime -lt
(Get-Date).AddDays(-$DaysOld)
    } | ForEach-Object {
        # Placeholder for now: Just display the file
to be deleted
        Write-Output "Target for Deletion:
$($_.FullName)"
    }
```

```
}
```

Explanation

1. `Get-ChildItem ... -File`: We efficiently fetch all files within the folder.
2. `Where-Object`: Our filter! It keeps only files whose `LastWriteTime` is older than the `DaysOld` threshold.
3. **(Placeholder Action):** For now, we're just *displaying* what *would* be deleted. Safety first!

Test Step: Basic Verification

Add this function to your script and try something like:

```
# ... Our existing functions from previous chapters
...

Verify-FolderPath -FolderPath 'C:\TestFolder' # A
folder with some old files
Process-FolderForCleanup -FolderPath 'C:\TestFolder'
-DaysOld 30
```

You should see a listing of files older than 30 days within the specified folder.

Why Start Simple?

- **Safety:** It's *crucial* to visually verify the logic selects the correct files before doing actual deletions.
- **Flexibility:** Our foundation lets us easily add more criteria later.

Key Concepts

- **Iteration:** Script development is often an iterative process, starting with simple logic, testing, and then expanding.
- **Pipelines:** We're leveraging the power of PowerShell pipelines to pass data between cmdlets for filtering and processing.

Practice

- **Create a Test Playground:** Set up a folder with files of known ages. Use it to experiment safely with your script's logic.

Up Next: From Display to Deletion

Now that we have a basic selection mechanism, we'll carefully introduce the actual file deletion process, along with essential safety measures like logging and perhaps a "what-if" mode.

Core Processing Logic – Part 2

Let's proceed with caution and enhance our core processing function to handle actual file deletion, while introducing essential safeguards to prevent accidental data loss.

From Display to Deletion

Inside your `Process-FolderForCleanup` function, replace the `Write-Output` line with the following:

```
Remove-Item -Path $_.FullName -WhatIf
```

- **Remove-Item:** This is the cmdlet responsible for deleting files.
- **-WhatIf:** This crucial parameter makes `Remove-Item` *describe* what it would do, without actually making changes.

Test: What-If Mode

Rerun your script from the previous chapter. Now, instead of just listing files, you should see actions like:

What if: Performing the operation "Remove File" on target "C:\TestFolder\OldDocument.txt"

Safety First! Always start with `-WhatIf`. Examine the output *very* carefully before proceeding.

Removing the Training Wheels

Once you're absolutely confident your file selection logic is correct, remove the `-WhatIf` parameter. **Caution:** This makes the script perform actual deletions!

Enhanced Logging

Let's add simple logging to track our script's actions:

```
# ... Inside the function ...
```

```
$logFile = Join-Path $FolderPath "Cleanup_Log.txt" #
Log file in the same folder

Get-ChildItem ... | Where-Object { ... } |
ForEach-Object {
    # ... (Our deletion logic with Remove-Item) ...
    "$(Get-Date) - Deleted: $($_.FullName)" |
Add-Content $logFile
}
```

Considerations

- **Real-World Logging:** Production scripts would use more structured logging, perhaps including deletion reasons (age, size, etc.).
- **Error Handling:** We haven't added `try/catch` blocks for file deletion yet. Robust scripts need this! (We'll cover this in-depth later)

Additional Resources

- **'WhatIf' Support:**
  https://docs.microsoft.com/en-us/powershell/module/microsoft.powershell.core/about/about_commonparameters

Practice

- **Intentional Mistake:** Temporarily introduce a small error into your age comparison logic. Run with `-WhatIf`, and observe how the script's reported actions clearly show the problem.

Adding More Criteria

Our core logic is functional, but basic! Let's illustrate how to add another criterion - file size:

```
# ... Inside the function ...
Get-ChildItem ... | Where-Object {
        $_.LastWriteTime -lt
(Get-Date).AddDays(-$DaysOld) -and
```

```
        $_.Length -gt 10MB  # Example: Files larger
than 10MB
    } | ForEach-Object {
        # ... Deletion and logging ...
    }
```

- **-and:** We combine conditions within our filter. Adapt the file size check as needed.

The Power of Combining Conditions

You can now target files based on age, size, file extensions... the possibilities are wide open!

Next: Wrapping Up Our Script

With the core logic in place, we're ready to put the finishing touches on our script, link it all together, and consider how we might execute it in real-world scenarios.

Core Processing Logic – Part 3

Let's put the final touches on our file cleanup script, address some real-world considerations, and discuss ways to execute it for practical use.

Review: Our Script So Far (Example)

```
# Parameters
param(
    [Parameter(Mandatory)]
    [string]$FolderPath,
    [int]$DaysOld = 30
)


# Function: Verify-FolderPath (from earlier
chapters)
# ...


# Function: Get-FolderStatistics (from earlier
chapters)
# ...


# Function: Process-FolderForCleanup
function Process-FolderForCleanup {
    # ... (Code from previous chapters) ...
}


# --- MAIN SCRIPT LOGIC ---

Verify-FolderPath -FolderPath "C:\SomeFolder"

$stats = Get-FolderStatistics -FolderPath
"C:\SomeFolder"
Write-Output $stats


Process-FolderForCleanup -FolderPath "C:\SomeFolder"
-DaysOld $DaysOld
```

Consolidating and Refinements

- **Top-Level Comments:** Add brief descriptions above each function and the main execution area for readability.
- **Output:** Do you want the cleanup log emailed? Written to a central file share? Adjust your script accordingly.

Making It Operational

Let's explore some ways to use your script:

1. **Manual Runs:** You could save it as `FileCleanup.ps1` and run it from the PowerShell ISE or terminal, providing the folder path when prompted.
2. **Scheduled Task:**
   - The Windows Task Scheduler can run PowerShell scripts on a schedule.
   - Useful for regular cleanup on critical folders.
   - Consider having the script send reports on its actions.
3. **Interactive Tool:** You could add more advanced parameters (confirmations, detailed filtering) and turn your script into a simple menu-driven tool for less technical users.

Real-World Considerations

- **"Undo" Is Hard:** File deletion is often irreversible. **Backups are your friend** if the target data is truly important.
- **Testing, Testing, Testing:** Use test folders and the `-WhatIf` parameter liberally during development.
- **Permissions:** The account running the script needs the rights to delete files in the target locations.

Additional Resources

- **Windows Task Scheduler:** [invalid URL removed]

Practice

- **Set Up a Test Task:** Use the Task Scheduler to run a simple PowerShell script (one that writes "Hello" to a file) at a specific time. This is good practice for operationalizing your cleanup script.

Beyond the Basics

Here are some ideas for expanding your script:

- **Archiving:** Instead of deleting, implement logic to move matching files to a designated archive folder based on a date.
- **File Types:** Add parameters to filter by file extension (`.log`, `.tmp`, etc.)
- **Presets:** Have "cleanup modes" – a 'conservative' vs. an 'aggressive' set of parameters for different scenarios.

The Power of Automation

Even a seemingly simple project like this demonstrates the core concepts of PowerShell automation: targeted actions, flexible parameters, and the ability to integrate with your existing IT systems.

Congratulations! You've built a valuable PowerShell tool and leveled up your scripting skills.

Final Script and Execution

Let's bring our file cleanup project to its culmination! In this chapter, we'll assemble the complete script, explore execution scenarios, and discuss some additional tips to ensure the script's success in real-world environments.

The Complete Script

Here's our script in its entirety, including functions and the main execution logic. Feel free to tailor this based on the features you've chosen to implement.

```powershell
# ------------------ Functions --------------------

function Verify-FolderPath {
    # ... (Code from earlier chapters) ...
}

function Get-FolderStatistics {
    # ... (Code from earlier chapters) ...
}

function Process-FolderForCleanup {
    param(
        [Parameter(Mandatory)]
        [string]$FolderPath,
        [int]$DaysOld = 30
    )

    $logFile = Join-Path $FolderPath
"Cleanup_Log.txt"

    Get-ChildItem -Path $FolderPath -Recurse -File |
Where-Object {
        $_.LastWriteTime -lt
(Get-Date).AddDays(-$DaysOld)
    } | ForEach-Object {
        Remove-Item -Path $_.FullName # No more
-WhatIf!
```

```
        "$(Get-Date) - Deleted: $($_.FullName)" |
Add-Content $logFile
    }
}


# ------------------ Main Script Logic
------------------


# Parameter input (in the ISE, or modify for a
scheduled task)
$FolderPath = "C:\Temp"
$DaysOld     = 14


# Verification
Verify-FolderPath -FolderPath $FolderPath


# Gather Statistics
$stats = Get-FolderStatistics -FolderPath
$FolderPath
Write-Output $stats


# Perform Cleanup
Process-FolderForCleanup -FolderPath $FolderPath
-DaysOld $DaysOld
```

Execution Scenarios

1. **Interactive (PowerShell ISE)**
   - Paste the entire script into the ISE.
   - Set the $FolderPath and $DaysOld variables at the bottom.
   - Run (F5) to execute the entire script.
2. **Command-Line / Terminal**
   - Save the script as FileCleanup.ps1.
   - Run: .\FileCleanup.ps1 -FolderPath "C:\SomePath" -DaysOld 7
3. **Scheduled Task**
   - Create a task in the Windows Task Scheduler.

- ○ Action: "Start a program"
- ○ Program: `powershell.exe`
- ○ Arguments: `-File "C:\Scripts\FileCleanup.ps1" -FolderPath "C:\ImportantData" -DaysOld 30`

Important Notes

- **Script Location:** Adjust paths in scheduled tasks if your script isn't in the root of `C:\`.
- **Logging:** Review the cleanup log file!
- **Permissions:** The executing account (you, or the scheduled task's user) needs permissions on the target folders.

Beyond the Basic Script

- **Error Handling:** Implement `try/catch` blocks, especially around file deletion, for more robust error reporting.
- **Email Reports:** Have the script send a summary email after each run, especially when used in scheduled tasks.
- **Advanced Parameters:** Control logging levels, create a "simulation mode" instead of deletion, etc.

Security Considerations

- **Principle of Least Privilege:** If possible, run scheduled tasks with an account that has *only* the permissions needed for the cleanup task.
- **Script Signing (Production):** For sensitive environments, consider signing your PowerShell scripts to prevent tampering.

Additional Resources

- **Robust Error Handling:** https://docs.microsoft.com/en-us/powershell/module/microsoft.powershell.core/about/about_try_catch_finally

Practice

- **Create a Scheduled Task:** Set up a task to run a basic PowerShell script, even one that just displays a message. This is invaluable practice for automating your cleanup script.

The Power of a Humble Script

What started as a simple idea has turned into a powerful automation tool. You now have the knowledge to solve real-world file management problems using PowerShell!

Congratulations! 🎉

Section 6:
PowerShell for System Administration

Working with Windows Services – Part 1

Let's dive into the world of Windows services! Understanding how to manage them with PowerShell is a crucial skill for any IT administrator or power user.

What are Windows Services?

- **Background Programs:** Services are a special type of program that run in the background, often without direct user interaction.
- **System Backbone:** They handle vital tasks like file sharing, printing, updates, remote access, and countless other essential functions.
- **Startup:** Many services are configured to start automatically when your Windows system boots.

Why PowerShell for Service Management?

1. **Efficiency:** PowerShell cmdlets let you manage multiple services on local or remote machines with a few lines of code.
2. **Automation:** Tasks like checking service status across servers or configuring services during setup can be easily automated with scripts.
3. **Integration:** PowerShell's ability to interact with other components of Windows (event logs, scheduled tasks) gives you a holistic control.

Key Cmdlets

Let's introduce the core cmdlets you'll be working with:

- **Get-Service:** The workhorse. Retrieves information about services. Can be filtered by name, status, and more.
- **Start-Service:** Starts a service.
- **Stop-Service:** Stops a running service.
- **Restart-Service:** Restarts a service.
- **Set-Service:** Changes a service's configuration (startup type, description, etc.)

Basic Exploration

1. **View All Services:** `Get-Service` (This might output a long list!)
2. **Filter by Name:** `Get-Service -Name Spooler` (Print Spooler service)
3. **See Running Services:** `Get-Service | Where-Object {$_.Status -eq 'Running'}`

Service Status

The 'Status' property is important:

- **Running:** The service is currently active.
- **Stopped:** The service is not running.
- **Other States:** Some services might have states like "Paused" or "Start Pending".

Managing a Service

Let's experiment with the "Print Spooler" service:

```
Stop-Service -Name Spooler
Get-Service -Name Spooler  # Verify it's stopped
Start-Service -Name Spooler
```

Important Note: Be cautious when stopping critical services, as this can disrupt system functionality. Always research a service before manipulating it!

Practice

1. **Find Services by State:** Get a list of all services that are *not* currently running.

2. **Remote Machine:** If you have access to another Windows machine on your network, use the `-ComputerName` parameter of the service cmdlets to manage it remotely.

Next Up: Advanced Control

We've scratched the surface. In the next part, we'll learn how to change service startup behavior, work with service dependencies, and delve deeper into filtering and customization with PowerShell's object-oriented magic.

Working with Windows Services – Part 2

Let's delve deeper into the realm of PowerShell service management, exploring advanced configuration and the power that comes from harnessing the object-oriented nature of PowerShell.

Service Startup Types

Each service has a startup type, which can usually be:

- **Automatic:** Starts when the system boots.
- **Manual:** Must be started manually by a user or another trigger.
- **Disabled:** Cannot be started.

Changing Startup Type (Set-Service)

```
Set-Service -Name spooler -StartupType Disabled
Get-Service -Name spooler # Verify the change
```

Use Cases

- **Troubleshooting:** Temporarily disable a suspect service to isolate problems.
- **Optimization:** Set infrequently used services to 'Manual' to potentially speed up boot times.
- **Security:** Disable non-essential services to reduce your system's attack surface.

Service Dependencies

Many services rely on others to function. For example, the 'Remote Desktop' service might depend on networking services being available.

Viewing Dependencies

```
Get-Service -Name "Remote Desktop Services" |
Select-Object -ExpandProperty DependentServices
```

Considerations

- **Be Thorough:** If you stop a service, its dependents will likely stop or malfunction as well.

- **Start Order:** Windows starts services taking dependencies into account.

PowerShell Objects to the Rescue

Filtering by Properties

```
Get-Service | Where-Object {$_.StartupType -eq
'Automatic' -and $_.Status -eq 'Stopped'}
```

This finds all services set to 'Automatic', but currently not running.

Custom Output

```
Get-Service Spooler, DHCPClient | Format-Table Name,
Status, StartupType -AutoSize
```

Additional Resources

- **'Set-Service':**
  https://docs.microsoft.com/en-us/powershell/module/microsoft.powershell.management/set-service

Practice

1. **Critical Service List:** Make a list of services that are set to 'Automatic' and are crucial for *your* system's operation.
2. **Start Them All!** Write a PowerShell line to start all services on a remote machine named 'RemoteServer' that are currently stopped. (`-ComputerName` parameter might be your friend!)

Real-World Applications

Let's imagine some administrative scenarios where these skills shine:

- **Server Setup:** A script to configure services on a new server – startup types, descriptions, etc. – ensures consistency.
- **Troubleshooting:** A script to check if vital services are running, and attempt to restart them if not.
- **Baselining:** A report detailing all non-standard services (not set to 'Automatic') across a network, aiding in security audits.

Beyond the Basics

A wealth of possibilities lies ahead:

- **Service Accounts:** Services often run under specific user accounts. PowerShell lets you manage those too.
- **Custom Service Creation:** Advanced users can create their own Windows services and manage them with PowerShell.

Mastery Through Practice

The more you experiment with managing services using PowerShell, the more it becomes second nature. This skillset is invaluable for streamlining administrative workflows.

Next Up: Tasks and Processes

Our next focus will be on managing running processes – starting, stopping, and understanding the resource usage of the programs powering your Windows systems.

Managing Processes and Tasks – Part 1

Let's embark on managing processes with PowerShell. Understanding how to control these core building blocks of a running system is a true hallmark of an IT administrator.

What is a Process?

- **Programs in Action:** When you run an application (your browser, a game, a background updater), it becomes a process.
- **Resources:** Each process consumes memory, CPU time, and may interact with files, the network, and other system resources.
- **Task Manager Analog:** Think of processes as what you see in the 'Details' tab of the Windows Task Manager, but supercharged!

PowerShell's Process Toolkit

Let's meet our primary cmdlets for process control:

- **Get-Process:** The powerhouse. Retrieves information about running processes.
- **Stop-Process:** Terminates one or more processes.
- **Start-Process:** Launches a new process (i.e., starts a program).
- **Wait-Process:** Pauses script execution until a process exits.

Basic Exploration

Let's get hands-on:

1. **See All Processes:** `Get-Process` (Prepare for a potentially long list)
2. **By Name:** `Get-Process -Name notepad`
3. **With IDs:** `Get-Process -Id 2684` (Substitute a process ID, or 'PID', you find on your system)

Understanding Process Output

`Get-Process` doesn't just give you names. You'll see properties like:

- **CPU:** Amount of processor time used.

- **WorkingSet:** Memory usage (in bytes).
- **Path:** Location of the executable file.
- **And many more!**

Stopping a Process

Use with caution! Stopping processes can disrupt your work.

- **By Name:** `Stop-Process -Name notepad -Force`
- **By ID:** `Stop-Process -Id 2684 -Force`

Note: Some processes may resist termination or require administrative privileges to stop.

Additional Resources

- **'Get-Process' Deep Dive:**
  https://docs.microsoft.com/en-us/powershell/module/microsoft.powershell.management/get-process
- **'Stop-Process':**
  https://docs.microsoft.com/en-us/powershell/module/microsoft.powershell.management/stop-process

Practice

1. **Resource Hog:** Use `Get-Process | Sort-Object WorkingSet -Descending` to find the process using the most memory on your system right now.
2. **Start a Program:** Try using `Start-Process` to launch a simple program like Calculator (`calc.exe`).

The Power of Filtering

Like with services, we can use `Where-Object` to get very specific with our process management:

```
# Example: Processes consuming too much CPU for a
long time
Get-Process | Where-Object {$_.CPU -gt 10 -and
$_.StartTime -lt (Get-Date).AddHours(-1) }
```

Use Cases

- **Runaway Scripts:** Terminate a misbehaving PowerShell script of your own.
- **Pre-update Cleanup:** Stop non-critical programs before an OS update to avoid conflicts.

Part 2: Going Deeper

Next, we'll learn how to discover relationships between processes, manipulate process windows, and explore techniques for automating tasks based on processes.

Managing Processes and Tasks – Part 2

Let's continue our process management journey, exploring advanced interactions and how PowerShell gives you fine-grained control over the tasks running on your systems.

Beyond the Basics

1. **Process Ownership:** Sometimes, it's crucial to know *who* or *what* launched a process. You can often discover this additional information with `Get-Process`. Look up extended property techniques online for the precise commands.
2. **Start-Process Variations:**
   - `Start-Process -FilePath "notepad.exe" -Verb RunAs` (Launch as administrator)
   - You can control the process's window state (minimized, maximized).

Parent-Child Relationships

Processes can spawn other processes. For example, your web browser might launch multiple subprocesses to handle different tabs. Exploration of these relationships can be helpful for troubleshooting.

It's sadly beyond the scope of this chapter to offer a single command that reveals everything, as it involves WMI queries. There are, however, excellent articles and scripts online on this topic.

Window Manipulation

While less common in pure system administration, sometimes you might need to interact with process windows:

```
# (Assuming notepad is running)
$notepadProcess = Get-Process -Name notepad
[void] $notepadProcess.MainWindowTitle # Get the
current window title
$notepadProcess.CloseMainWindow()      # Minimize
(if possible)
```

Caution: These manipulations can be disruptive to the user!

Waiting for Processes

Use cases include scripts that must perform an action *after* another program finishes.

```
Start-Process notepad.exe -PassThru | Wait-Process
# At this point, Notepad has closed and the script
continues
```

Real-World Applications

- **Update Orchestration:** A script to install updates might:
    1. Stop a critical service cleanly.
    2. Launch the updater program.
    3. `Wait-Process` on the updater.
    4. Restart the service.
- **Monitoring:** A script that periodically checks if a specific process is running, restarting it if not, and potentially sending an email alert.

Additional Resources

- **Window Manipulation (Limited):**
  https://docs.microsoft.com/en-us/dotnet/api/system.diagnostics.process

Practice

1. **Resilient Notepad:** Write a short script that launches Notepad. If Notepad closes unexpectedly, it relaunches it. (Hint: a loop and `Get-Process` might help!)

Bridging the Gap: Scheduled Tasks

PowerShell can manage the Windows Task Scheduler! Cmdlets exist to create, modify, and run scheduled tasks. This integration is immensely powerful:

- **Automation Triggers:** Run PowerShell scripts on a schedule, not just at times you manually invoke them.

Notes

- A full Task Scheduler lesson is out of our current scope. Focused chapters would do this justice.
- Search online for PowerShell Task Scheduler cmdlets to start learning.

PowerShell as the Task Master

We've only scratched the surface of process control. The ability to query, launch, terminate, and interact with the core 'living' elements of your operating system positions you as a true IT maestro

Next Up: System Performance

Shifting our focus, the next chapters will arm you with the tools to monitor the overall health and performance metrics of your Windows machines using PowerShell.

Monitoring System Performance – Part 1

Let's dive into the world of system performance monitoring with PowerShell. Understanding how to gauge the health and resource usage of your Windows machines is an essential skill for any administrator or power user.

Why Does Performance Matter?

- **Troubleshooting Bottlenecks:** Is your system slow? Identifying the culprit (disk, CPU, memory) is the first step towards a solution.
- **Proactive Monitoring:** Establishing baselines and watching for trends can help you prevent problems before they cause downtime.
- **Capacity Planning:** Are your servers powerful enough to handle future workloads? Performance data informs these decisions.

PowerShell Performance Toolkit

PowerShell offers several ways to access system performance metrics:

1. **Performance Counters:** Windows exposes a vast array of real-time performance data through 'counters'. PowerShell has cmdlets to tap into these.
2. **WMI:** Windows Management Instrumentation is a repository of system information. PowerShell can query WMI for performance data (and much more).
3. **.NET Classes:** For certain specialized metrics, you can directly access .NET Framework functionality from within PowerShell.

Let's Start with Performance Counters

- **General Counter Exploration:** `Get-Counter -ListSet *` (This might produce a *lot* of output)
- **Paths:** Counters are organized in a `\Category\Subcategory\Instance` format. Example: `\Processor(_Total)\% Idle Time`

Using Get-Counter

```
Get-Counter -Counter "\Memory\Available MBytes"
-SampleInterval 2 -MaxSamples 5
```

- **\Memory\Available MBytes:** Gets the available system memory.
- **SampleInterval:** How often to take a reading (seconds).
- **MaxSamples:** How many readings to gather.

Focusing Your Monitoring

It's rarely useful to monitor *everything*. Common targets include:

- **CPU:** \Processor(_Total)\% Processor Time
- **Memory:** \Memory\% Committed Bytes In Use, \Memory\Available MBytes
- **Disk:** \LogicalDisk(*)\Avg. Disk Queue Length, \LogicalDisk(*)\% Free Space
- **Network:** \Network Interface(*)\Bytes Received/Sec, \Network Interface(*)\Bytes Sent/Sec

Additional Resources

- **Performance Counter Basics:** https://docs.microsoft.com/en-us/windows/win32/perfctrs/about-performance-counters

Practice

1. **Current CPU Load:** Get a single reading of the \Processor(_Total)\% Processor Time counter.
2. **Disk Space Check:** Find the percent free space on your C: drive.

Practical Use Cases

- **Quick System Glance:** A one-line PowerShell command to get the current CPU, free memory, and disk space on a remote system.
- **Basic Logging:** A script that samples key counters every few minutes and writes the data to a CSV file for trend analysis.

Part 2: Going Further

Next, we'll look at retrieving more complex performance data using WMI, how to format the output, and ways to visualize performance trends over time.

Monitoring System Performance – Part 2

In this chapter, we'll delve into WMI queries, enhance output formatting, and discuss ways to visualize the performance data you collect.

WMI: The Powerhouse of System Data

1. **Beyond Counters:** WMI offers a treasure trove of information, including hardware details, software configuration, and much more.
2. **The 'Get-WmiObject' Cmdlet:** This is our gateway to querying WMI.

Example: Detailed Memory Information

```
Get-WmiObject -Class Win32_OperatingSystem |
Select-Object TotalVisibleMemorySize,
FreePhysicalMemory
```

- **Win32_OperatingSystem:** A common WMI class containing OS-level data.

Discovering WMI Classes

1. **Online:** Search for things like "WMI Win32 Classes List" for extensive documentation.
2. **Get-WmiObject Exploration:** Get-WmiObject -List will display available classes (be prepared for a long output)

Output Formatting

So far, our output has been raw. Let's improve this:

```
Get-Counter "\Processor(_Total)\% Processor Time"
-SampleInterval 1 -MaxSamples 5 |
    Format-Table -Property Timestamp, CounterSamples
```

- **Format-Table:** Arranges data in a tabular format.
- **Select-Object:** (Used earlier) Lets you choose only relevant properties to display.

Practical Performance Scripts

Here's a more complete example:

```
function Get-SystemSnapshot {
    Get-Counter -Counter '\Memory\% Committed Bytes
In Use', `
                        '\Memory\Available MBytes',
`
                        '\Processor(_Total)\%
Processor Time' |
        Format-Table -AutoSize -Property Timestamp,
CounterSamples
}


# Get a few snapshots with a pause in-between
Get-SystemSnapshot
Start-Sleep -Seconds 5
Get-SystemSnapshot
```

Visualizing Performance Data

1. **Simple Graphing:** PowerShell modules like 'PSChart' exist, but they may have a learning curve.
2. **Logging and Excel:** Often the most practical. Log performance data to a CSV, then use Excel's powerful charting features.
3. **Dedicated Monitoring Tools:** For large environments, consider tools like Zabbix, or Grafana – these can use PowerShell as a data source.

Additional Resources

- **WMI Reference:**
  https://docs.microsoft.com/en-us/windows/win32/wmisdk/wmi-classes

Practice

1. **Disk Info:** Use `Get-WmiObject` to find the model and size of your hard drives.
2. **Logged Trend:** Modify the script above to log several snapshots to a CSV file over a longer duration.

Key Takeaways

- PowerShell gives you flexible ways to tap into various sources of performance data.
- Even simple scripts can be powerful aids in detecting and analyzing system behavior.

Up Next: The Windows Event Log

Our next focus will be on the Windows Event Log, a rich source of information for troubleshooting errors, security auditing, and understanding what's happening beneath the surface of your systems.

PowerShell and Event Logs – Part 1

Let's unlock the secrets held within the Windows Event Log. Understanding how to work with event logs using PowerShell is a hallmark of a skilled systems administrator.

What is the Windows Event Log?

- **The System's Diary:** A structured record of events generated by the operating system, applications, and services.
- **Types of Events:** Informational, warnings, errors, audit successes/failures…
- **Event Logs:** Think of them as categorized sub-diaries. Common ones include 'Application', 'System', 'Security'.

Why PowerShell for Event Logs?

- **Log Size:** The GUI Event Viewer can be slow with large logs.
- **Filtering Power:** PowerShell lets you pinpoint the exact events you need with laser precision.
- **Remote Access:** Query events on other machines for centralized monitoring.

Introducing the Cmdlets

- **Get-EventLog:** The workhorse. Retrieves event log entries.
- **Clear-EventLog:** Clears events from a log. (Use with caution!)
- **Write-EventLog:** Lets you create your own custom event log entries.
- **Limit-EventLog:** A newer alternative for some scenarios

Basic Exploration

1. **List Available Logs:** `Get-EventLog -List`
2. **Recent System Events:** `Get-EventLog -LogName System -Newest 10`
3. **Errors Only:** `Get-EventLog -LogName Application -EntryType Error`

The Anatomy of an Event

Event log entries have numerous properties. Some important ones:

- **EntryType:** (Error, Warning, etc.)
- **TimeGenerated:** When the event occurred.
- **Source:** The component that generated the event.
- **EventID:** A numeric code *unique within a source.*
- **Message:** The descriptive text (this can be long!).

Practice

1. **Critical Errors:** Find all events with 'EntryType' of 'Critical' from the past 24 hours on your system.
2. **Event Sources:** Get a list of all the unique 'Source' names found in your 'Application' log.

Filtering Event Logs

This is where PowerShell truly shines:

```
# Events from a specific service failing to start
Get-EventLog -LogName System -Source "Service
Control Manager" -InstanceId 7036


# Events in a time range
$startTime = (Get-Date).AddDays(-1)
Get-EventLog -LogName System -EntryType Error -After
$startTime
```

Part 2: Going Deeper

Next, we'll delve into advanced filtering using XPath queries, interpreting the message text of events, and how to streamline event log analysis for real-world problem-solving.

PowerShell and Event Logs – Part 2

Let's continue our journey into the world of Event Log analysis with PowerShell. In this chapter, we'll cover advanced filtering techniques, making sense of event messages, and automating routine log-related tasks.

Advanced Filtering with XPath

1. **Beyond Simple Properties:** XPath is a query language for XML-like data. Event Logs have some internal structure that XPath lets you target.
2. **Example:** Finding events where a specific process ID is mentioned within the event data:

```
Get-EventLog -LogName System -FilterXPath
"*[EventData[Data[@Name='ProcessID'] = '4']] "
```

Note: XPath syntax can get complex. Start with simple queries and build from there.

Demystifying Event Messages

Often, the most valuable information is in the 'Message' property of an event. Unfortunately, these can be:

- **Long and Cryptic:** Filled with codes and placeholders for data.
- **Source-Specific:** The same Event ID might have *different* messages depending on the software that generated it.

Tactics

1. **Online Search:** Search for the Source, EventID, and snippets of the message. You'll often find explanations on forums or vendor documentation.
2. **Experimentation (Carefully):** If possible, intentionally trigger the event in a test environment to examine its message.

Formatting Event Data

Let's make event messages easier to digest:

```
Get-EventLog -LogName System -Newest 5 |
    Format-List EntryType, TimeGenerated, Source,
EventID, Message
```

Note: Some messages may still be long. PowerShell's automatic wrapping in the console can help.

Practical Use Cases

Let's look at some targeted scenarios:

- **Security Auditing:** A script to check the 'Security' log daily for failed logon attempts, sending a summary email.
- **Troubleshooting a Service:** Filter for events from your service's 'Source', potentially correlating them with performance counters to spot issues.
- **Change Tracking:** Many events log configuration changes. A script to report on these across servers could be an audit trail.

Beyond the Basics

- **Remote Event Logs:** The -ComputerName parameter of the Event Log cmdlets lets you query other machines on your network.
- **Custom Event Writing:** Use Write-EventLog in your scripts to log important actions for later analysis.
- **Specialized Modules:** There are PowerShell modules that further enhance your ability to work with Event Logs in complex ways.

Additional Resources

- **Event Log WevtUtil:** (Advanced command-line tool, complementary to PowerShell)
  https://docs.microsoft.com/en-us/windows-server/administration/windows-commands/wevtutil

Practice

1. **Specific Event:** See if you can construct a Get-EventLog command (using XPath if needed) to isolate a *very* particular kind of event in your logs.

Power to the Administrator

The ability to harness the Windows Event Logs with PowerShell gives you deep insights. This knowledge is crucial for troubleshooting problems, staying on top of security, and ensuring the smooth operation of your IT systems.

Continuing the Journey

The topics of PowerShell-driven automation, error handling, creating robust scripts… all these general skills become even more potent when combined with the system knowledge you've gained in these systems administration chapters.

Managing Scheduled Tasks – Part 1

Why Scheduled Tasks?

- **Automation:** Run scripts, programs, or commands on a schedule – daily backups, system maintenance, etc.
- **Triggers:** Flexible scheduling options – time-based, at system startup, when idle, in response to events…
- **Centralization:** The Task Scheduler is a built-in Windows component where you manage these automated actions.

Why Manage Tasks with PowerShell?

- **Consistency:** Scripts to create tasks ensure the same settings across multiple machines.
- **Remote Management:** Control tasks on other systems you have administrative rights to.
- **Integration:** Tasks can be part of larger PowerShell workflows, their results acted upon, and so on.

PowerShell's Toolkit

PowerShell has a dedicated module for scheduled tasks since Windows Server 2012/Windows 8 and onwards:

- **Module Name:** ScheduledTasks
- **Key Cmdlets:** Let's explore these later, but they include getting task info, creating tasks, modifying, running, and deleting them.

Note: For older Windows versions, there are ways to interact with scheduled tasks (the 'schtasks' command, COM objects), but they are less convenient than the PowerShell module.

Let's Get Started!

1. **Import the Module:** `Import-Module ScheduledTasks`
2. **See Existing Tasks:** `Get-ScheduledTask` (But be prepared for potentially numerous results)
3. **Task Details:** `Get-ScheduledTask -TaskName "MyTaskName" | Select-Object *` (Reveals *many* properties)

Properties of a Scheduled Task

Some commonly used properties include:

- **TaskName:** What the task is called.
- **State:** Is it enabled, ready to run, disabled?
- **Triggers:** What causes the task to execute.
- **Actions:** What the task actually *does*.
- **Principal:** The user account the task runs as.

Filtering Tasks

```
# Tasks set to run only when the user is logged on
Get-ScheduledTask | Where-Object
{$_.Principal.LogonType -eq "InteractiveToken"}


# Tasks from a specific folder
Get-ScheduledTask -TaskPath "\Microsoft\Windows\"
```

Additional Resources

- **ScheduledTasks Module Docs:**
  https://docs.microsoft.com/en-us/powershell/module/scheduledtasks

Practice

1. **Disabled Tasks:** Get a list of all the scheduled tasks on your system that are currently in the "Disabled" state.
2. **Last Run:** Find the last time a specific task executed successfully. (Hint: look at the `LastRunTime` property)

Part 2: Creating and Modifying Tasks

In the next chapter, we'll delve into the heart of task management: creating tasks from scratch, configuring their every detail, and modifying existing ones – all through the power of PowerShell!

Managing Scheduled Tasks – Part 2

Let's continue our exploration of scheduled task management with PowerShell. In this chapter, we'll create new tasks, modify every aspect of existing ones, and learn how to orchestrate them for our administrative needs.

Creating a New Scheduled Task

The heart of this process is the New-ScheduledTaskAction, New-ScheduledTaskTrigger, and New-ScheduledTask cmdlets. Let's build a basic example:

```
# 1. Action: What to execute
$action = New-ScheduledTaskAction -Execute
"notepad.exe"


# 2. Trigger: When to run
$trigger = New-ScheduledTaskTrigger -Once -At
(Get-Date).AddMinutes(2)


# 3. The Task Itself
$task = New-ScheduledTask -Action $action -Trigger
$trigger -Description "Demo Task"


# 4. Register (Create) the Task
Register-ScheduledTask -TaskName "MyDemoTask"
-InputObject $task
```

Task Settings

You can create intricate tasks using additional cmdlets from the ScheduledTasks module. Example:

```
$settings = New-ScheduledTaskSettingsSet
$settings.AllowStartIfOnBatteries = $false  # Only
run if on AC power
Register-ScheduledTask -TaskName ... -Settings
$settings
```

Modifying a Task

1. **Get the Task:** `$task = Get-ScheduledTask -TaskName "MyTask"`
2. **Modify Properties:** You now have a task object. Change things like `$task.Triggers`, `$task.Actions`, etc.
3. **Update:** `Set-ScheduledTask -InputObject $task`

Example: Disable a Task

```
$myTask = Get-ScheduledTask -TaskName "MyTask"
$myTask.State = "Disabled"
Set-ScheduledTask -InputObject $myTask
```

Controlling Task Execution

- **Start-ScheduledTask:** Immediately run a task.
- **Stop-ScheduledTask:** Stop a currently running task.
- **Unregister-ScheduledTask** Delete a task (use with caution!)

Real-World Applications

- **Update Script Task:** A script creates a task to run itself on a later schedule for automated updates.
- **Cleanup Tasks:** A task to delete old log files, triggered weekly.
- **Conditional Execution:** A task triggers another task *only* if certain criteria are met (e.g., a service is in a failed state).

Practice

1. **Daily Report:** Create a scheduled task that runs a simple PowerShell script every day at a specific time. The script should generate a text file summary of available disk space.
2. **Change a Trigger:** Modify an existing scheduled task to run monthly instead of weekly.

Tips

- **Test Thoroughly:** Especially if modifying tasks crucial to your systems, test your PowerShell changes in a non-production environment first.

- **Remote Machines:** Use the -ComputerName parameter on the ScheduledTasks cmdlets to manage tasks on other systems you have administrative access to.

Beyond the Basics

The ScheduledTasks module provides even more granular control over task security contexts, idle conditions, repetition intervals… the possibilities are extensive!

Integration Power

Remember, PowerShell scheduled task management is but one tool in your automation arsenal. Combining tasks with your knowledge of services, processes, and event logs opens the doors to truly intelligent and self-maintaining systems.

Section 7:
PowerShell Automation and Advanced Techniques

Working with REST APIs in PowerShell – Part 1

Let's understand REST APIs and how PowerShell empowers you to interact with them, extending your automation capabilities far beyond your local systems.

Understanding REST APIs

- **The Backbone of Modern Web:** REST (Representational State Transfer) is an architectural style, a standardized way for web services to communicate.
- **Data Exchange:** APIs let you retrieve data (like weather, stock prices), or send instructions (update a social media post).
- **Language of the Web:** They predominantly use the HTTP protocol and often exchange data in the JSON format (which PowerShell loves).

Why Use REST APIs with PowerShell?

1. **Beyond Your Domain:** Interact with cloud services, third-party platforms, IoT devices, and any system that exposes a REST API.
2. **Automate the Web:** Turn web-based tasks you'd normally do manually into automated scripts, saving time and reducing errors
3. **Mashups:** Combine data or actions from multiple services to create unique workflows tailored to your needs.

PowerShell's Primary Tool: `Invoke-RestMethod`

This is your workhorse cmdlet. Let's see it in action:

```
$weatherData = Invoke-RestMethod -Uri
"https://api.openweathermap.org/data/2.5/weather?q=L
ondon&appid=YOUR_API_KEY"

$weatherData.main.temp  # Access the temperature
data
```

Things to Know

- **URI:** The 'address' of the API endpoint.
- **Methods:** REST APIs use HTTP methods – GET (fetch data), POST (send data), and others. `Invoke-RestMethod` figures this out partly from context.
- **Authentication:** Many APIs need an API Key, or use other authentication methods. How to do this depends on the specific API.

API Exploration

Before scripting, you'll need these details from the API's documentation:

1. **Endpoint URIs:** The addresses for different *kinds* of data or actions.
2. **Parameters:** What input the API expects (city names, dates, etc.)
3. **Data Structure:** How the JSON (or sometimes XML) response is organized.

Additional Resources

- `Invoke-RestMethod`:
  https://docs.microsoft.com/en-us/powershell/module/microsoft.powershell.utility/invoke-restmethod

Practice

1. **Public APIs:** Find a fun public API (a list is at https://github.com/public-apis/public-apis) and try fetching some data.

Part 2: Real-World Use and Advanced Techniques

In the next chapter, we'll dive into practical examples of automating interactions with cloud services, sending data to APIs, handling errors, and parsing more complex JSON responses.

Working with REST APIs in PowerShell – Part 2

Let's continue our journey into harnessing REST APIs with PowerShell. In this chapter, we'll tackle real-world examples, sending data, handling complex responses, and even touch upon error handling.

Real-World Example: Controlling IoT Devices

Let's say you have smart light bulbs with a REST API. Documentation might look like this:

- **Change Color:**
  - POST `https://api.smartbulbs.com/bulb/123/state`
  - Body (JSON): `{"color": "blue"}`

PowerShell Code:

```
$bulbId = "123"
$body = @{ color = "red" } | ConvertTo-Json
Invoke-RestMethod -Uri
"https://api.smartbulbs.com/bulb/$bulbId/state"
-Method Post -Body $body -ContentType
"application/json"
```

Observations

- `ConvertTo-Json`: Turns a PowerShell hashtable into JSON data.
- `-ContentType`: Tells the API we're sending JSON.

Sending Data (Beyond GET)

Often APIs need more than a URL. Let's imagine a translation service:

- POST `https://api.translate.com/translate`
- Body (JSON): `{"text": "Hello World", "targetLang": "es"}`

```
$parameters = @{
    text = "Hello World"
    targetLang = "es"
}
```

```
Invoke-RestMethod -Uri
"https://api.translate.com/translate" -Method Post
-Body (ConvertTo-Json $parameters)
```

Parsing JSON Responses

APIs usually send back JSON. Use `ConvertFrom-Json`:

```
$response = Invoke-RestMethod ...
$jsonObj = $response | ConvertFrom-Json
$jsonObj.translatedText # Might contain the result
```

Caution: JSON structures can be nested! Explore the data with `$jsonObj | Get-Member`

Error Handling

Things *will* go wrong with APIs: bad requests, authentication issues…

- **Invoke-RestMethod:** May throw exceptions. Look into PowerShell's `try/catch` for robust scripts.
- **HTTP Status Codes:** The API often includes a status code in the response indicating success, failure, etc.

Additional Resources

- **JSON in PowerShell:** https://docs.microsoft.com/en-us/powershell/module/microsoft.powershell.utility/convertfrom-json

Practice

- **Modify the API Examples:** Pretend the API examples above require an API key as a header, something like `-Headers @{`

`'X-API-Key' = 'your_key_here' }`. Change the PowerShell code accordingly.

Going Beyond the Basics

- **Authentication:** APIs may use OAuth or other complex schemes. PowerShell can handle this but requires more in-depth study.
- **Large Datasets:** Consider advanced JSON parsing for complex responses.
- **Asynchronous Calls:** For efficiency, learn how to make API calls without 'blocking' your script's execution.

Unlocking Integration Power

The ability to interact with systems and services through REST APIs expands the horizons of your PowerShell automation. Imagine scripts that:

- **Post server monitoring alerts to your communication platform (Slack, etc.)**
- **Pull data from a CRM system and generate a nicely formatted PowerShell report**
- **Control a home automation setup based on schedules or external events**

Let's continue!

Interacting with Azure Services – Part 1

Let's venture into the realm of managing cloud resources with PowerShell, specifically focusing on Microsoft's Azure platform.

Why PowerShell for Azure?

- **Automation & Consistency:** Create, configure, and control Azure resources through scripts. Ideal for repeatability and infrastructure-as-code.
- **Integration:** PowerShell scripts can be part of larger workflows, using Azure output as input for other systems, and vice-versa.
- **Cross-Platform:** PowerShell's availability on Windows, macOS, and Linux lets you manage Azure from anywhere.

Prerequisites

1. **Azure Subscription:** You'll need a valid Azure account to practice the examples. (There might be a free trial option)
2. **The Az Module:**
   - Install it with `Install-Module -Name Az -AllowClobber`
   - Import it: `Import-Module Az`

Fundamentals: Connecting to Azure

Use the `Connect-AzAccount` cmdlet. Here's an interactive way:

1. Run `Connect-AzAccount`
2. You'll be prompted to authenticate in a web browser.

Note: There are advanced connection methods (service principals) for non-interactive scenarios, but we'll keep it simple for now.

Exploring Azure with Cmdlets

The 'Az' module has a *lot* of cmdlets. Patterns to know:

- **Nouns:** Cmdlets follow a 'Verb-AzNoun' structure. Examples:
   - `Get-AzVM` (List virtual machines)

- ○ `New-AzResourceGroup` (Create a resource group)
- ○ `Stop-AzWebApp` (Stop a web app)

Getting Help

- **`Get-Help <cmdlet-name>`:** Always your first line of defense.
- **Az Module Reference:** See [invalid URL removed]

Basic Tasks

Let's try some core actions:

- **List Resource Groups:** `Get-AzResourceGroup`
- **Create a Resource Group:**
  `New-AzResourceGroup -Name "MyTestGroup"`
  `-Location "EastUS"`
- **Create a Virtual Machine (VM):** This can get complex! Look at the extensive parameters of the `New-AzVM` cmdlet for all the options.

Practice

1. **List Azure Subscriptions:** If you have multiple subscriptions tied to your account, use cmdlets to list them.
2. **Explore a Cmdlet:** Run `Get-Help New-AzVM -Detailed` to see the sheer number of options involved in creating a VM.

Part 2: Real-World Use Cases

Next, we'll look at automating common Azure tasks:

- **Provisioning Infrastructure:** Scripts to deploy VMs, networks, storage, etc., based on parameters.
- **Monitoring:** Check the health or status of Azure resources.
- **Scaling:** Scripts reacting to load/metrics to add/remove Azure resources.

Security Considerations

- Avoid storing Azure credentials in plain text within scripts. Use secure mechanisms like Azure KeyVault. We may cover such topics in a later secure scripting chapter.

The Power of Cloud Automation

Mastering Azure PowerShell interaction unlocks a world of efficient cloud management. You gain the ability to codify your infrastructure, spin up resources on-demand, and build intelligent systems that respond dynamically to the needs of your workloads.

Interacting with Azure Services – Part 2

Let's continue our journey into managing Azure with PowerShell! In this chapter, we'll delve into practical scenarios, automating common tasks, and ensuring our scripts interact with Azure efficiently.

Real-World Automation Scenarios

1. **Provisioning a Web App:**

```
# Parameters
$rgName = "MyResourceGroup"
$location = "WestUS2"
$appName = "MyWebApp"

# Create Resource Group if it doesn't exist
if (-not (Get-AzResourceGroup -Name $rgName)) {
    New-AzResourceGroup -Name $rgName -Location
$location
}

# Create an App Service Plan (for hosting the
web app)
New-AzAppServicePlan -Name "MyPlan" -Location
$location `
                     -ResourceGroupName $rgName
-Tier "Basic"

# Create the Web App
New-AzWebApp -Name $appName -Location $location
`
             -ResourceGroupName $rgName
-AppServicePlan "MyPlan"
```

2. **Scheduled VM Backups:** A script using Azure VM backup cmdlets, triggered by a scheduled task.
3. **Cost Reporting:** Generate a CSV report of Azure resource usage for a billing period, providing insights into spending.

Beyond the Basics

- **Filtering with Azure PowerShell:** Many 'Get-Az...' cmdlets let you filter server-side:
  ```
  Get-AzVM -ResourceGroupName "ProductionVMs"
  ```
- **Piping Azure Objects:** Output from one cmdlet can be piped into the next for chained actions.
- **Azure PowerShell Profiles:** Settings to make logins persistent across sessions (see 'Az.Accounts' module).

Efficiency Considerations

- **Batching:** Some Azure cmdlets support batch operations, making changes to multiple resources more efficient.
- **Asynchronous:** Research the 'Az' module's asynchronous features for long-running tasks to avoid blocking your script.

Real-World Example: Scaling a Web App

Imagine load-based scaling:

1. **Monitor Metrics:** Use Azure cmdlets (or REST API calls) to get web app's CPU usage.
2. **Decision Logic:** If the CPU is above a threshold *and* the app is not already at its max instance count...
3. **Scale Up:** Use cmdlets like `Update-AzWebApp` to increase instances/size of an Azure Web App.

Additional Resources

- **Azure PowerShell Advanced Functions:** Some tasks have helper functions to simplify them, like `Publish-AzWebApp`. Search the documentation!

Practice

- **Modify VM Size:** Write a script to find a VM by name and update its size (look at VM size options in the Azure portal for valid values).

Security Note

Production Azure scripts often need more sophisticated authentication methods than interactive logins. Service Principals and Managed Identities are concepts to research for more robust deployments.

The Power of Azure Automation

By combining your Azure PowerShell knowledge with:

- **Scheduled Tasks:** Run scripts on a timed basis.
- **Webhooks:** Trigger scripts from Azure alerts or external systems.
- **Azure Functions:** Serverless code to execute your PowerShell.

…you can create truly dynamic and responsive cloud infrastructure management!

Next Steps

PowerShell and Azure are a vast topic. Consider exploring:

- **Azure Automation:** A service dedicated to running PowerShell in the cloud
- **ARM Templates:** For complex deployments in a declarative JSON format
- **The Azure CLI:** A cross-platform alternative to PowerShell cmdlets

Let's continue refining your automation abilities!

Integrating PowerShell with Other Tools – Part 1

Let's explore the powerful concept of integrating PowerShell with other tools, expanding the boundaries of your automation and problem-solving abilities.

Why Integration?

1. **Leverage Existing Tools:** PowerShell is rarely the *only* tool you'll need. Integrating it with specialized software lets each component do what it does best.
2. **End-to-End Workflows:** Break large automation tasks into smaller steps, using the right tool for each stage, with PowerShell as the orchestrator.
3. **Extend PowerShell's Reach:** PowerShell, by itself, might not be able to control every system or device. Integration bridges those gaps.

Methods of Integration

Let's look at the most common ways you'll connect PowerShell to the outside world:

1. **Command-line Execution:**
   - PowerShell can run executables (programs, scripts in other languages...).
   - Capture output: Text sent to standard output by the external tool can be used in your PowerShell script.
   - **Example:** `$ipAddress = ipconfig | Where-Object { $_ -match "IPv4" }` (Assumes 'ipconfig' works on your system)
2. **APIs (REST and Others):**
   - We've covered REST APIs in detail.
   - Sometimes tools expose legacy SOAP APIs, or custom ones. PowerShell can often work with these (though it might get more complex).
3. **Libraries and .NET:**

- o PowerShell can load .NET assemblies. If a tool has a .NET SDK, this unlocks direct interaction via objects.
- o **Example:** A C# DLL for controlling a niche hardware device could be used from PowerShell.

4. **Databases:**
   - o PowerShell has cmdlets for some database systems (e.g., SQL Server).
   - o More commonly, you'd use .NET for database connections, executing queries, and processing the results.

Real-World Scenarios

1. **Network Device Configuration:**
   - o A PowerShell script to:
     - Read a CSV of device IPs and config changes
     - Use vendor-provided CLI tools, invoked from PowerShell, to push changes to each device.

2. **Ticketing System Integration**
   - o PowerShell monitors an event log.
   - o On certain events, it calls the API of a ticketing system to create a new ticket with relevant details

3. **Reporting with Excel:**
   - o PowerShell gathers data (system info, Azure costs, etc.)
   - o It utilizes .NET to automate Excel, create a nicely formatted workbook, and email it.

Additional Resources

- **Tool-Specific Documentation:** The best resources will often be the docs for the tool you're integrating *with*. Look for API references, command-line usage, or .NET SDKs.

Practice

- **Test CLI Integration:** If you have the 'ping' command available, run `ping 8.8.8.8` from PowerShell and capture the output lines. Parse them to get basic ping statistics.

Part 2: Deeper Dives and Challenges

In the next chapter, we'll cover:

- Passing data between PowerShell and external tools in structured formats (like JSON).
- More advanced .NET integration techniques.
- Potential issues like handling long-running external processes.

Key Takeaways

- PowerShell is rarely an island. Its ability to connect with other technologies is a superpower for the resourceful administrator.
- Integration projects often require learning a bit about the external system – its API style, command-line tools, etc.

Integrating PowerShell with Other Tools – Part 2

Let's continue expanding PowerShell's capabilities by integrating it even more deeply with external tools and systems.

Passing Structured Data (Beyond Text)

Often, you'll need to exchange more complex information than simple command-line output:

1. **CSV:**
   - PowerShell is great at CSV. External tools might accept CSV input or produce it.
   - Cmdlets: `Import-Csv`, `Export-Csv`
2. **JSON:**
   - Very common for modern tools having APIs.
   - PowerShell Cmdlets: `ConvertTo-Json`, `ConvertFrom-Json`

Example: CSV Device Configuration

```
$deviceConfig = Import-Csv "devices.csv"
foreach ($device in $deviceConfig) {
    # Assume 'Set-DeviceConfig' is a command from a vendor
tool
    Set-DeviceConfig -Hostname $device.Hostname -Setting
$device.Setting -Value $device.Value
}
```

Using .NET for Deeper Integration

PowerShell's ability to leverage the .NET Framework is immensely powerful for integration tasks:

1. **Loading .NET Assemblies:** `Add-Type -Path "PathToYourAssembly.dll"`
2. **Creating .NET Objects:** `$excel = New-Object -ComObject Excel.Application`

3. **Calling Methods, Properties:** `$excel.Visible = $true`

Example: Generating an Excel Report

```
Add-Type -AssemblyName
Microsoft.Office.Interop.Excel
$excel = New-Object -ComObject Excel.Application
# ... Add Workbooks, Worksheets, Populate Cells ...
$excel.SaveAs("MyReport.xlsx")
$excel.Quit()
```

Caution

- .NET is huge; you'll need to research the object model for the tool you're integrating with.
- COM Objects (older tech) can be finicky, but sometimes the only way to interact with a legacy system.

Managing Long-Running Processes

- **Background Jobs:** Use PowerShell jobs (Look up `Start-Job`) to run external tasks without blocking your main script.
- **Timeouts:** Consider ways to terminate misbehaving external processes, as PowerShell might be stuck waiting for them to finish.

Additional Resources

- **.NET Documentation:** https://docs.microsoft.com/en-us/dotnet/ – especially if interacting with .NET APIs from a vendor.

Practice

- **JSON + REST:** If you can find a public API that returns data in JSON format (many exist), try fetching it with PowerShell and then displaying the results in a meaningful way.

Challenges of Integration

- **Documentation:** The quality of documentation for the tool you're integrating with will massively affect the ease of the project.

- **Versioning:** Changes in an API or a tool's command-line interface can break your carefully crafted scripts.

The Best of Both Worlds

PowerShell's integration abilities enable you to orchestrate workflows that seamlessly utilize:

- PowerShell's text manipulation, file handling, etc.
- Specialized vendor tools
- Web services
- Legacy systems with oddball interfaces

The more you practice this kind of integration, the more complex automation scenarios you'll be able to tackle.

Next Up

The next step on our PowerShell mastery journey is the creation of reusable modules to neatly package your PowerShell code and create shareable libraries of functions!

Building Custom Modules in PowerShell – Part 1

Let's delve into the world of building your own PowerShell modules, a crucial step in mastering scripting and creating well-organized, reusable PowerShell tools.

Why Create Modules?

1. **Organization:** Break large scripts down into focused modules. Easier to manage and maintain.
2. **Reusability:** Functions you define in a module are available in *any* PowerShell session once you import it. Stop copy-pasting code!
3. **Sharing:** Modules let you create libraries of functions for your team, yourself on other machines, or even the wider PowerShell community.

Types of Modules

- **Script Modules (.psm1):** The most common type. Contains PowerShell functions, primarily.
- **Manifest Modules (.psd1):** Includes a manifest file describing the module's contents, author, version, and more.
- **Binary Modules (.dll):** Contain compiled C# code. Advanced, but provide performance or access to low-level features. We'll focus on script modules first.

Module Basics: Creating Your First Module

1. **Module File:** Create a file named MyCustomModule.psm1.
2. **A Simple Function:** Inside the .psm1 file:

```
function Get-Uptime {
    $startTime = (Get-Date).Subtract($bootTime)
# Assumes you have a global $bootTime
    "System has been up for: $startTime"
}
```

3. **Saving the Module:** Place `MyCustomModule.psm1` in a directory within your PowerShell Module Path. Check the `$env:PSModulePath` variable to see these locations.
4. **Import:** `Import-Module MyCustomModule`
5. **Usage:** `Get-Uptime` is now a usable cmdlet!

Module Structure – Best Practices

- **Functions:** Each module should ideally have a set of related functions. A module to manage network shares, one for Azure interactions, etc.
- **Naming:** Function names should be Verb-Noun, just like PowerShell cmdlets.

Exporting Functions

By default, every function you define in a .psm1 is NOT made available when you import. Let's fix that:

1. **Inside your .psm1:** At the bottom, add:

```
Export-ModuleMember -Function Get-Uptime
```

Now, only `Get-Uptime` will be usable after importing.

Additional Resources

- **'about_Modules'** : Run `Get-Help about_Modules` within PowerShell for in-depth documentation.

Practice - Extend the Uptime Module: Add a function to your module that calculates uptime in a more visually appealing format (days, hours, minutes).

Part 2: Manifests, Help, and Distribution

In the next chapter, we'll cover:

- **Module Manifests:** Metadata for your module, enabling features like versioning.

- **Writing Help for Your Functions:** So users (and future you!) know how to utilize your custom cmdlets.
- **Module Distribution:** Basics of sharing your modules.

The Power of Modularization

Creating custom PowerShell modules is a hallmark of a skilled PowerShell practitioner. It elevates your scripts into structured, reusable components that accelerate your automation journey!

Building Custom Modules in PowerShell – Part 2

In this chapter, we'll go deeper, adding module manifests, incorporating help for your functions, and touch upon sharing your creations.

Module Manifests (.psd1)

1. **What:** A `.psd1` file defines metadata and advanced settings for your module.
2. **Create one:** In the same folder as your `.psm1` create a file named `MyCustomModule.psd1`
3. **Basic Structure:**

```
New-ModuleManifest -Path .\MyCustomModule.psd1
-Author "Your Name" -RootModule
"MyCustomModule.psm1"
```

4. **Benefits (many!)**
   - Versioning
   - Defining dependencies on other modules
   - Control what functions are *automatically* exported
   - …and more

Writing Help for Your Functions

Make your modules user-friendly! PowerShell has a comment-based help system:

```
<#
.SYNOPSIS
Calculates system uptime in a friendly format.

.DESCRIPTION
Provides uptime in days, hours, minutes, seconds.

.EXAMPLE
Get-FriendlyUptime
```

```
#>
function Get-FriendlyUptime {
    # ... Your function code here ...
}
```

Accessing Help

- `Get-Help Get-FriendlyUptime` – Shows your help
- `Get-Help Get-FriendlyUptime -Detailed` – Even more!

Best Practices for Help

- **Write it as you code:** Easier to keep it up-to-date.
- Include examples!

Module Distribution Basics

While there are sophisticated ways to package modules, here's a simple start:

1. **Central Location:** A file share accessible to machines where you want to use the module.
2. **PSModulePath:** Temporarily add this file share to the `$env:PSModulePath` of target machines. Your module becomes importable.

Note: Robust distribution might involve creating a PowerShell Gallery repository (internal or on the public internet). A topic for a later chapter, perhaps!

Practice

1. **Add a Manifest:** Create a basic `.psd1` manifest for your uptime module.
2. **Help Extravaganza:** Write detailed help for all the functions within your module.

Beyond the Basics

A few things we haven't touched on yet, but are important for serious module development:

- **Source Control:** Use Git (or similar) for versioning and tracking changes to your modules.
- **Automated Testing:** Pester is a PowerShell testing framework to ensure your modules work as expected.
- **Advanced Module Types:** We focused on script modules; there's more!

Empowering Reusability and Structure

By mastering module creation, you gain the ability to:

- Build libraries of tools tailored to your specific environments and tasks.
- Share code between your scripts, promoting consistency and reducing redundancy.
- Collaborate effectively on PowerShell projects within teams.

Let's continue honing your PowerShell skills, tackling topics like error handling and debugging next!

Error Handling and Debugging – Part 1

Let's embark on a crucial aspect of PowerShell mastery: the art of error handling and debugging. Understanding how to anticipate problems, write robust scripts, and troubleshoot effectively will significantly enhance your automation abilities.

Why Does Everything Break?

- **External Factors:** A network share disappears, a file is missing, an API changes its response… things outside your script's direct control.
- **Mistakes Happen:** Typos, incorrect assumptions about input data, or simply changes in your environment over time.
- **Complexity:** The more intricate your script, the more places for things to go wrong.

Types of Errors

1. **Terminating Errors:** These halt your script abruptly. Often displayed in red text. Example: trying to access a file that doesn't exist.
2. **Non-Terminating Errors:** Your script continues, but results might be incorrect, or actions incomplete. These can be trickier to spot!

PowerShell's Error Stream

Cmdlets, and your own functions, report errors on a separate "channel" – the error stream. This is key to error handling!

The $Error Automatic Variable

PowerShell keeps a list of recent errors in $Error. Let's cause one on purpose:

```
Get-Item NoSuchFile
$Error[0]  # View the most recent error
```

Note: $Error is an array; there might be multiple errors.

`try/catch` – The Cornerstone of Error Handling

```
try {
    Get-Item NoSuchFile  # A statement that might
fail
} catch {
    Write-Warning "File not found!"
    # Do something else: log an error, try an
alternative, etc.
}
```

- **The `try` Block:** Code where you suspect issues could occur.
- **The `catch` Block:** Runs ONLY if an error happens in the `try` block.

Finally (Optional)

Add a `finally` block to your `try/catch`. This code *always* runs, error or not, useful for cleanup tasks.

Additional Resources

- **about_Try_Catch_Finally:** Get-Help about_Try_Catch_Finally

Practice - Safe File Copy: Modify a simple file copying script to use `try/catch`, providing a user-friendly message if either the source or destination is invalid.

Part 2: Debugging, Error Types, and Customization

Next, we'll delve into:

- **Debugging Techniques:** Stepping through your code, examining variables. (A bit of the PowerShell ISE will help here)
- **Common Error Types:** Understanding 'CommandNotFoundException', 'ItemNotFoundException', and how to catch them specifically.
- **Customizing Error Behavior:** The `-ErrorAction` parameter on cmdlets and `$ErrorActionPreference` for broader control.

Key Takeaways

- Errors *will* occur. The goal is to make your scripts resilient and provide informative messages when things go awry.
- Proactive error handling separates a polished PowerShell script from a fragile one.

Let's continue refining your PowerShell problem-solving toolkit!

Error Handling and Debugging – Part 2

Debugging Techniques

The PowerShell ISE offers some useful tools. Demo time! (But the same concepts apply broadly)

1. **Breakpoints**
   - Click in the left margin of your script to set a red dot (breakpoint).
   - Run your script. It will pause *before* executing the line with the breakpoint.
2. **Investigating at a Breakpoint**
   - Examine variables: `Get-Variable`, or hover over variables in code
   - Step-through: F10 (over), F11 (into functions), Shift-F11 (out)
   - The console is live! Manually test commands at the breakpoint.

Common Error Types to Catch

You can fine-tune error handling:

```
try {
    Get-ChildItem NoSuchPath
} catch [System.IO.DirectoryNotFoundException] {
    "That directory doesn't exist"
} catch {
    "Some other error happened: $_"  # General
catch-all
}
```

- **Know Your Cmdlets:** Each cmdlet can throw specific exceptions. Docs often list them.

Customizing Error Behavior

1. **ErrorAction Parameter**
   Many cmdlets have it: `Get-Item -ErrorAction`

`SilentlyContinue` suppresses the error in that case. Other options are 'Stop', 'Ignore'...

2. **$ErrorActionPreference**
   This global variable sets a default behavior for your script or session. ('Stop' makes scripts terminate on errors more often, good for debugging sometimes).

Logging for Later

Instead of just displaying errors, consider *writing them to a file*:

```
catch {
    "Error on $(Get-Date):  $_" | Add-Content
error.log
}
```

Advanced Tip: Write-Error vs. Throw

- `Write-Error` is for non-terminating errors, things you want to report but continue.
- `throw` generates terminating errors. Use it in your own functions to signal serious problems.

Additional Resources

- **Write-Error:**
  https://docs.microsoft.com/en-us/powershell/module/microsoft.powershell.utility/write-error

Practice

1. **Intentional Bug:** Introduce a mistake into a working script (e.g., rename a variable that's used later). Use the ISE to step through and pinpoint the issue.
2. **Log It:** Add a `catch` block that logs errors from a file operation, including a timestamp and the full path that was problematic.

Beyond the Basics

- **Remote Debugging:** Debug scripts running on other computers!

- **Error Records:** The $Error variable has rich details beyond the basic message.
- **Custom Error Objects:** Advanced, but lets you get very structured for error handling in your modules.

The Importance of Debugging

The ability to systematically isolate and fix issues has multiple benefits:

- **Resilient Scripts:** Your automation runs smoothly *despite* the unpredictability of the real world.
- **Your Own Understanding:** Debugging forces you to understand your code's logic deeply.
- **Collaboration:** Well-debugged scripts are easier for others (and future you!) to maintain.

A Continuous Learning Process

Error handling and debugging are skills honed with practice. As you build more complex PowerShell projects, the investment you make in these areas will pay dividends in the reliability and maintainability of your work!

Deploying PowerShell Scripts Securely – Part 1

Let's delve into a crucial aspect of real-world PowerShell usage: secure script deployment. Moving from scripts that work on *your* machine to reliable, secure automation solutions requires careful consideration.

Why Does Security Matter?

- **Malicious Alteration:** If your powerful script falls into the wrong hands, modifications could cause damage to systems.
- **Accidental Mistakes:** Even well-intentioned users might run scripts in incorrect contexts, or make changes without fully understanding the consequences.
- **Credentials:** Scripts often need credentials to access resources. Exposing these credentials is a major risk!

Security Considerations

We'll focus on a few key areas:

1. **Script Signing**
   - Digital signatures help verify the script's origin and whether it's been tampered with.
   - Requires using certificates (New-SelfSignedCertificate, or from a Certificate Authority in more regulated environments).
   - **Execution Policy:** PowerShell's execution policy can be configured to require signed scripts.
2. **Secure Credential Storage**
   - **Don't hardcode them!** Hardcoded credentials in scripts are easily found.
   - **Windows Credential Manager:** A built-in option for storing them more securely.
   - **Solutions like:** Azure KeyVault, Hashicorp Vault, etc., are designed for secrets.
3. **Least Privilege**
   - Does the script *need* to run with admin rights?

○ If possible, use accounts with only the permissions necessary for the task. This limits the potential damage if something goes wrong.

Example: Signing a Script

1. **Certificate:** Assuming you've created one for code signing...
2. **Set-AuthenticodeSignature:**

```
$cert = Get-ChildItem Cert:\CurrentUser\My
-CodeSigningCert
Set-AuthenticodeSignature -FilePath
"MyScript.ps1" -Certificate $cert
```

Execution Policies

- Run `Get-ExecutionPolicy -List` to see policies for different scopes.
- 'Restricted' is the default (disallows scripts).
- 'RemoteSigned' is a good middle ground - locally authored scripts work, downloaded ones require signing.

Important: Execution policy is *not* foolproof security. It's a part of your defense-in-depth strategy.

Additional Resources

- **Signing Cmdlets:**
  https://docs.microsoft.com/en-us/powershell/module/microsoft.powershell.security/set-authenticodesignature

Practice - Inspect a Signature: If you have a signed script, use `Get-AuthenticodeSignature` to examine it.

Part 2: Going Deeper

Next time, we'll cover:

- **Credential Management Tools:** How to use the Windows Credential Manager from PowerShell, and considerations for more advanced secret vaults.

- **Encryption at Rest:** For scripts containing sensitive sections, even if the whole script can't be signed.
- **Auditing and Logging:** Tracking who ran what script and when.

Important Notes

- **Security is Contextual:** The right level for a home lab is different from a highly regulated enterprise environment.
- **Stay Up-to-Date:** Vulnerabilities and best practices evolve, so revisit your security measures over time.

Deploying PowerShell Scripts Securely – Part 2

Let's continue our discussion on making your PowerShell automation robust and secure in real-world environments.

Managing Credentials

1. **Windows Credential Manager**
   - Built into Windows. Suitable for less-critical use cases.
   - **Cmdlets:** `Get-Credential`, `New-StoredCredential`
   - **Demo:**

   ```
   $cred = Get-Credential
   $cred | New-StoredCredential -Target
   "MyScript"
   # Later...
   $retrievedCred = Get-StoredCredential
   -Target "MyScript"
   ```

2. **Dedicated Secrets Vaults**
   - Examples: Azure KeyVault, Hashicorp Vault, others.
   - Stronger security features (fine-grained access controls, auditing)
   - May have their own PowerShell modules for interaction.

Tip: Search the PowerShell Gallery (https://www.powershellgallery.com/) for modules tailored to your secrets management tool.

Limiting Exposure: Script Parameters

Avoid hardcoding credentials even within `New-StoredCredential`. Instead:

```
# In your script
Param(
    [PSCredential] $ScriptCredential
)
```

```
# Do things with $ScriptCredential
```

Now, provide credentials at runtime – command-line, a GUI prompt for the user, or from a calling system.

Encryption at Rest

For sensitive code blocks within scripts:

1. **ConvertTo-SecureString**
   - Input a normal string, output is obfuscated (not true security, but a deterrent)
2. **Protect-CmsMessage / Unprotect-CmsMessage**
   - True encryption, but tied to the user/machine where it was done.

Auditing and Logging

- **Script Transcript:** Use `Start-Transcript` and `Stop-Transcript` to capture script output. Vital for forensics.
- **Centralized Logging:** Send key actions from your scripts to a log aggregation system (many options exist – ELK Stack, Splunk, cloud-based services, etc.)

Practice

Store and Retrieve: Using the Windows Credential Manager, store credentials for a fictitious external system. Then practice retrieving them within a script.

Beyond the Basics

- **Just-In-Time Access:** Credentials granted temporarily, via a privileged access management (PAM) solution.
- **Hardware Security Modules (HSM):** Specialized devices for key storage, used in high-security environments.
- **Threat Modeling:** Analyze your scripts to see where the most sensitive points for attack might be. This influences your security choices.

Important Considerations

- **No Silver Bullet:** There's no single solution that's perfect for everyone.
- **Defense in Depth:** Signing, least privilege, credential management, logging… all form layers of security.
- **Usability vs. Security:** A balance is needed, too much security makes scripts hard to actually use.

The Evolving Security Landscape

PowerShell, as a powerful automation tool, is an attractive target. It's crucial to:

- Keep your PowerShell knowledge up-to-date (new versions might have security enhancements).
- Follow security best practices as they evolve.

Conclusion

Throughout your journey with PowerShell, you have unraveled a world of possibilities for those who work with systems, both large and small. What started with simple commands has blossomed into a robust toolkit for tackling the intricate challenges of the IT landscape and beyond.

Key Takeaways

- **Automation Mindset:** PowerShell instills a philosophy of efficiency. Each task becomes an opportunity to streamline, save time, and reduce human error.
- **Object Mastery:** Understanding how PowerShell sees the world – as objects with properties and methods – unlocks flexible data manipulation and problem-solving techniques.
- **Integration Power:** Rarely is PowerShell an island. Its ability to connect with REST APIs, Azure, legacy systems, and specialized tools makes it the glue of modern IT operations.
- **Problem-Solving Weapon:** From file organization to cloud orchestration, your scripts become precision instruments to resolve recurring issues and provide insights.

The Path Continues

Your mastery of PowerShell is not a destination, but an ongoing journey. Remember:

- **The Community:** Tap into the vibrant PowerShell community online for help, pre-built solutions, and insights into cutting-edge techniques.
- **PowerShell Evolves:** New versions, modules, and best practices emerge. Stay curious and keep your skills sharp.
- **Real-World Projects:** The true measure of your expertise lies in applying PowerShell to solve problems you care about - at work, at home, or for the sheer joy of creation.

Think, Automate, Empower

Whether you're a seasoned IT professional or a power user seeking to transcend the limitations of manual work, PowerShell has equipped you with new ways to think, new strategies to automate, and most importantly, the power to shape your digital world.

Every time you confidently fire up the PowerShell console, remember that with a few lines of code, you have the ability to:

- Tame the tedium, leaving precious time for higher-level work.

- Bring consistency and control to complex systems.
- Uncover insights hidden within oceans of data.
- Build solutions others will marvel at.

Go Forth and Automate!

The world is in constant flux, technology ever-changing… The need for the elegant automation that you can design with PowerShell will only grow. Take pride in the skills you've honed, embrace the challenges ahead, and above all – keep automating!